"Every book on adoption or foster care that I've ever encountered was a theological treatise or a personal memoir or a how-to manual. *Called to Care* is the first book on this topic that has it all—heartfelt stories, spiritual reflection, a range of perspectives, and heaps of practical advice. This book is a veritable one-stop shop for anyone who is interested in or thinking about orphan care, and it is written by two of the most respected and trustworthy adoption advocates of the last quarter century in America. If you take seriously the Bible's commands to care for orphans, read this book immediately."

—Jonathan Merritt, contributing writer, the *Atlantic*, and author, *Learning to Speak God from Scratch: Why Sacred Words Are Vanishing—and How We Can Revive Them*

"When God calls you to step into the lives of children, he'll also prepare you. This practical, informative guide helps do just that. The short stories, questions, and prayers at the end of each chapter will lead you to a deeper dialogue with God—then watch where God takes you!"

—Dr. Sharen E. Ford, director, Foster Care and Adoption, Focus on the Family

"Bill Blacquiere reminds us that the family is the building block of society in God's design. Finding families for children through foster care, adoption in all its forms, and strengthening families is the clarion call he invites us to respond to in the third decade of the twenty-first century."

—Albert L. Reyes, president and CEO, Buckner International

"I highly recommend this as a mandatory read for anyone considering adoption, foster care, or working with vulnerable children."

—Michael Douris, president, Orphan Outreach

CALLED TO
CARE

CALLED TO
CARE

Opening Your Heart to Vulnerable Children—through
Foster Care, Adoption, and Other Life-Giving Ways

BILL BLACQUIERE

WITH KRIS FAASSE

BETHANYHOUSE
a division of Baker Publishing Group
Minneapolis, Minnesota

© 2019 by Bethany Christian Services, Inc.

Published by Bethany House Publishers
11400 Hampshire Avenue South
Bloomington, Minnesota 55438
www.bethanyhouse.com

Bethany House Publishers is a division of
Baker Publishing Group, Grand Rapids, Michigan

Printed in the United States of America

Library of Congress Cataloging-in-Publication Data
Names: Blacquiere, Bill, author. | Faasse, Kris, author.
Title: Called to care : opening your heart to vulnerable children through foster care, adoption, and other life-giving ways / Bill Blacquiere with Kris Faasse.
Description: Bloomington, Minnesota : Bethany House Publishers, 2019. | Includes bibliographical references.
Identifiers: LCCN 2019019123| ISBN 9780764233340 (trade paper : alk. paper) | ISBN 9781493421831 (e-book)
Subjects: LCSH: Church work with adoptive parents. | Adoption—Religious Aspects—Christianity. | Foster parents. | Adoptive parents.
Classification: LCC BV4529.15 .B33 2019 | DDC 259/.22—dc23
LC record available at https://lccn.loc.gov/2019019123

The stories in this book have been drawn from real people and their journeys. Most names and some of the narratives, however, have been changed or adjusted to protect the privacy of individuals and families or highlight the various aspects of the call to care.

Cover design by Brand Navigation

Authors represented by Verne Kenney

19   20   21   22   23   24   25   7   6   5   4   3   2   1

Bill

To foster and adoptive families for older children and children with placement challenges and host families with Safe Families for Children. These families are the real heroes in caring for children, and without them the system would crash. They give of their time, emotional health, and financial resources to help children. Their passion and zeal for the children they care for is abundant. Despite the challenges, their response is "I will care for more children."

Kris

This book is dedicated to those children and families without a voice, those who have responded to them, and the Bethany staff, who, from our founding, have cared deeply and sought to be the hands and feet of Christ.

Contents

Introduction

Why This Book Is for You

Family is God's design—the place he created for children to be nurtured, to grow, and to mature, whether in their family of origin or in a new family.

In the United States and around the world, however, millions of children are at risk. They no longer have a family, or their family is unable to care for them the way they need. In some cases, children and their families don't have the help and support necessary to move through challenging times and stay together. Crisis or poverty—or both and even war—take their toll, and children can suffer. The late Dr. Karyn Purvis, cofounder of the Karyn Purvis Institute of Child Development at Texas Christian University in Fort Worth, Texas, called them "children from hard places."[1]

God calls us all to care for these most vulnerable among us by acting on their behalf. That's what *Called to Care* is about. This book will not only lay out God's call but will help you discover what answering his call might mean for you. If you're wondering how you personally fit into his plan for these children, this book is for you. If you're wondering how you might be called to serve other than as a foster or adoptive parent—although you might discover that *is* your call—this book is for you. And if you're wondering how your church or small group can embrace a meaningful role in answer to this call, this book is for you as well.

In these pages we'll share about the worldwide effort to support children who are among those the Bible calls "the least of these"—from neglected and abused children in America's cities to pregnant teenagers in America's heartland, from AIDS orphans in Africa to hurricane orphans in Haiti, from trafficked children in Cambodia to abandoned girls in China.

How do we know so much about these populations? Because transforming lives through the call to serve vulnerable children has been Bethany Christian Services' sole aim since its beginnings more than seventy years ago. Bethany's mission is to demonstrate the love and compassion of Jesus Christ by protecting and empowering children and youth and families through quality social services.

Bethany is driven to care for parents, both married and single, and their children who need help; refugees, orphans, and neglected and abused children; and children who have experienced multiple traumas in their lives. Bethany serves people in circumstances that range from heartbreaking to joyous and in cases that move like clockwork to those that are messy and slowgoing. And with every case its staff and volunteers experience God's grace and love through those helped.

But because God calls all his followers to be part of the worldwide effort to help vulnerable children find safe and loving homes, to help them heal from their hurts and traumas, and to assist the families and professionals in their lives, you have a personal call as well.

Yes, you might be called to be a foster parent or to adopt a child. Or you might be called to offer financial support or respite care. You might be called to simply pray. Whatever your specific call, if you're ready for God to reveal it, we believe he will.

We invite you to use the inspirational stories, compelling information, and practical tools throughout this book to help you discover how God has uniquely called you to open your heart and make a difference. The well-being—and in many cases the lives—of the most vulnerable children in his kingdom depends on all of us.

How to Use This Book

This book has four parts.

Part One: Examining the Call to Care describes the biblical call, how answering it differs for everyone, and how we can best prepare before we answer.

Part Two: Exploring Foster Care and Adoption unpacks these two traditional options for caring and their many forms.

Part Three: Embracing Family Preservation outlines actions and programs that help both families of origin and newly formed families stay together.

Part Four: Enriching Family Ties covers how families and friends, churches, and communities can step up to make a difference in the health of a family.

You can read all four parts from beginning to end for the broadest understanding of the call to care and how you might be called to answer. Or you can focus on one part or even one chapter you think will speak to you personally, wherever you are in this quest right now. Your approach is up to you.

Take note, too, of these features:

- **Opening Your Heart** suggests questions or ideas at the end of each chapter to guide you in processing, embracing, and acting on what you've read.

- **Praying for My Call** at the end of each chapter helps you begin asking God for understanding, peace, and guidance as you consider your, or perhaps your church's, answer to the call to care.

- **Appendices** in the back of the book offer resources for adoptive and foster parents and some Bethany-specific information.

Lastly, although most of the stories and scenarios you'll read have been drawn from Bethany experiences, and although some Bethany-specific information is in this book, remember that many organizations, agencies, and churches around the world are answering God's call to care for vulnerable children. Look for them wherever you are.

PART ONE

EXAMINING THE CALL TO CARE

1

What God's Word Says

To fully understand the call to care for vulnerable children, we need to research God's Word. The Bible calls us to care for the lonely, fatherless, widows, orphans, and the people Jesus called "the least of these." But before we examine some key passages, let's explore what the Bible tells us about family preservation.

Family Preservation

Family preservation is highlighted throughout the Christian Bible. Both the Old and New Testaments list family lineages—from Adam to Noah, from Noah to David, and from David to Jesus Christ. The lists of descendants reflect God's emphasis on preserving family. None of those people was perfect except Jesus, and some of them were downright dysfunctional (think of Judah having children with his daughter-in-law, Tamar, and King David having a son, Solomon, whose mother, Bathsheba, was the wife of Uriah).

Old Testament laws even provided ways for family lines to continue after a man died without children. Consider the story of Ruth and Naomi. Ruth, a non-Jewish woman, had married Mahlon, a Jewish man, who died childless. The widow Ruth followed her mother-in-law, Naomi, back to Israel, where Ruth married Boaz, a member of Mahlon's extended family and whose mother was the harlot Rahab who helped the Israelites at Jericho.

Boaz was excited. He said, "I have also acquired Ruth the Moabite, Mahlon's widow, as my wife, in order to maintain the name of the dead with his property, so that his name will not disappear from among his family or from his hometown. Today you are witnesses!" (Ruth 4:10).

All these people were in the lineage of Jesus, showing how God can redeem and use every child and person for his glory.

For Whom Are We Called to Care?

Three passages of Scripture particularly lay out God's call for us to care for the most vulnerable among us—and for us to recognize who those most vulnerable are.

The first is from King David, the beloved psalmist:

> Sing to God, sing in praise of his name,
> extol him who rides on the clouds;
> rejoice before him—his name is the Lord.
> A father to the fatherless, a defender of widows,
> is God in his holy dwelling.
> God sets the lonely in families,
> he leads out the prisoners with singing;
> but the rebellious live in a sun-scorched land.
>
> Psalm 68:4–6

Don't you love the phrase "God sets the lonely in families"? That's what we're called to do: set vulnerable children into families that love and care for them. Whether the families are permanent or temporary, the goal is to love, care for, and protect children.

James tells us,

Religion that God our Father accepts as pure and faultless is this: to look after orphans and widows in their distress and to keep oneself from being polluted by the world.

James 1:27

Jesus loved to tell a story, drawing in those who came to hear his teaching. His stories challenged the entrenched thinking of listeners, offending some, but his message was always clear. He told us about the importance of the call to care in the book of Matthew:

When the Son of Man comes in his glory, and all the angels with him, he will sit on his glorious throne. All the nations will be gathered before him, and he will separate the people one from another as a shepherd separates the sheep from the goats. He will put the sheep on his right and the goats on his left. . . .

Then the righteous will answer him, "Lord, when did we see you hungry and feed you, or thirsty and give you something to drink? When did we see you a stranger and invite you in, or needing clothes and clothe you? When did we see you sick or in prison and go to visit you?"

The King will reply, "Truly I tell you, whatever you did for one of the least of these brothers and sisters of mine, you did for me."

Matthew 25:31–33, 37–40

A father to the fatherless.
God sets the lonely in families.
Look after orphans and widows.
The least of these.

All these phrases speak to the biblical mandate to care for vulnerable children and families. All these ideas undergird the preservation of families, whether families of origin or those newly created.

Important to note is that when we reference "the least of these," we're not thinking of ourselves as better or superior, but we're living out our Christian calling to serve our brothers and sisters, equal to us in the eyes of God. "The least of these" are individuals without a voice, but when they are children placed in a family, they have someone to speak for them.

What Does Serving "the Least of These" Look Like Today?

Here are just two examples of how lives can change when the call to care is answered. In one story, a new family is formed. In the other, an existing family is preserved through a national program we'll talk more about later—Safe Families for Children (SFFC).

Mai, a single woman, had a busy life, but she also wanted to be a mother. She applied for foster care adoption and prayed about possible placements. Then she received a call about an eight-year-old girl.

"Are you afraid?" Mai asked Katie when she picked her up.

"No," she answered. That response marked the beginning of Mai's understanding of how much this little girl had been affected by neglect, abuse, and being "passed around."

After a brief time away as Mai became licensed for foster care adoption, Katie was returned to her care as a foster and pre-adoptive placement. Mai didn't know if Katie was hers to adopt or if she would be placed elsewhere, but a judge decided Katie would thrive best in a home like Mai's. Mai became her mom.

Katie leads an active life—she plays an instrument and is involved with dance, school, and church—and she's part of Mai's large extended family and has many cousins.

• • •

Holden was depressed, unemployed, and homeless—and solely responsible for his six-year-old son. They had no support system or church family, and Holden knew living out of his car wasn't safe for his boy.

Though it was a hard call to make, on Christmas morning he called Bethany Christian Services for help. The worker emailed the need to a list of families specially trained and willing to take children into their care temporarily and immediately received a response. The Safe Families for Children host family met Holden and his son at a gas station on their way to visit extended family, and the boy went with them. He stayed with them until Holden secured a job and housing.

The host family built a relationship with the pair throughout the little boy's stay. They invited Holden to church, and he began attending with them. He and his son still attend, and Holden is closer to God and his son than ever before. What could have been a tragic crisis developed into a transformative relationship.

Look beyond what you might think you know about helping the poor. For instance, most of the people living in poverty are women and children. And a recent survey by the *Washington Post* and the Kaiser Family Foundation found that white evangelical Christians are twice as likely to blame someone's poverty on "lack of effort," compared to non-Christians who say "difficult circumstances" cause poverty.[1]

Millions of people are in poverty, yet many of them work as hard or harder than those in the middle or upper classes. This is an example of how we must be educated to fully understand the call to care.

We are also to help those who are particularly endangered. For instance, children and families in refugee camps are malnourished. Many of the children in refugee camps have lost one or both parents, experienced hunger, been raped, been sexually assaulted, and witnessed siblings tortured, killed, and kidnapped. Conditions are poor, and some living there are naked. Water is available, but only if one can carry a five-gallon jerrycan. Refugee camps are like prisons, with fences and gates and nowhere else to go. It's not uncommon for children to spend their entire childhood in places like this. Consider, too, the children and teens who are or have been bound in slavery of all kinds.

Before we move from the biblical foundation for this call to care to what can motivate someone to answer that call, take in these inspiring stories. The first is about a couple who searched for and found the best way for them to answer their call to care, and the second is a first-person account from a refugee who intends to answer the call to care himself.

Larry and Mona had two biological children and considered expanding their family through adoption. Adoption, however, wasn't the best choice for them because they needed to financially protect the future of their daughter with physical challenges. Then they found the perfect fit for them.

They have cared for nine refugee teenage girls from all over the world, all of whom call them Mom and Dad. Mona calls the girls, who are between the ages of fifteen and twenty, "my kids." They arrived broken, having lost hope, homes, and family members in some cases. Some left family behind, and some arrived ill, but they all began to thrive in this loving, healthy environment.

Language differences weren't the test Larry and Mona expected because the teens grasped English quickly and their agency provided a contact person from each girl's country and counseling with translators. Yet routines like going to school were hard because many lived in refugee camps where their only job was survival. Food was also an issue because many of the girls faced real hunger and near starvation. Mona learned to keep a pot of cooked rice on the stove to help alleviate their fears of not having enough to eat.

"Reaping rewards can take a while," Mona said, "but our greatest reward has been watching the girls change and grow."

• • •

I grew up in what I would call "survival mode." When you are in survival mode, your focus is on getting through the day in one piece.

I never had a chance to be with my family; I never had a happy moment when I was a boy. I have no pictures I can look back on and see my family and memories. It's so painful, heartbreaking, and hopeless to be in this position. I wish you knew how it hurts. I wish you knew that I am not a burden; I just had bad luck because of my country and government. I *did not* choose to be a refugee or immigrant.

But I have hope, faith, and the courage to persevere and rebuild my shattered life. I tell my story not because it is unique, but because it is not a lone voice. I am many. I am me, but I'm also those millions of refugee children, teenagers, and adults.

College will help me be successful in studying psychology and international relations so I can become a refugee worker. I know only too well the plight of refugees and appreciate the efforts of various organizations to save lives, making a difference and a future where there is none.

Thank you to those lovely people who opened the door for me and continue to open the door for my fellow refugees and immigrants; thank you for your kindness. Thank you for showing me how to love deeply, thank you for feeding me and clothing me, and most importantly, may God bless you all. Everything you did for me I try to continue to do.

The Mandate Is Clear

The biblical mandate is clear: We are called to extend grace to others. For organizations like Bethany, and for all those who hear the call to care for children, that mandate means specific action to help them. A family is where children are healed. In healthy families, children who have come from hard places can heal their souls, their hearts, and their hurts. We all have the basic need to belong and feel secure, and families provide the emotional security of knowing "I belong." The goal is to be a bridge between children and families in many ways and places.

But no one can do it alone, least of all organizations, and God never intended them to. He wants individuals to answer the call he has for them.

Here's another story about answering the call to care through Safe Families for Children. Note how many individuals and groups answered the call to assist this one woman and her children who needed help.

When Deborah called SFFC, she asked for someone to care for her daughter when she went to the hospital to give birth to her second child. She had no family or friends.

Finding an Answer That Works for You

Bringing vulnerable children into our homes is often our first thought when we consider how we can answer the call to care. Don't necessarily dismiss that potential call until you've taken in the information outlined in this book and explored the options, but we're not all called to care in the same way.

If after careful consideration and prayer you know adoption, foster care, and refugee care don't fit your circumstances, at least for now, consider answering the call in other ways. Here are some examples:

- Commit to praying daily for a family waiting for an adoptive placement.
- Lead a prayer group that prays specifically for those working to protect children in the United States and abroad.
- Offer to grocery shop or pay for a grocery delivery service for a foster family who just welcomed a sibling group into their home.
- Prepare a care bag for a child entering foster care with age-appropriate underwear, socks, hygiene items, and books.
- Offer an afternoon of free childcare to an adoptive family.
- Financially support a family care center overseas, a local nonprofit that helps place children in foster homes, or an organization that helps care for children and families.
- Purchase and pack school items, clothing, toys, and so on for travelers to take overseas to family care centers.
- Serve in your church's classes for children with special needs so parents can worship in the service.
- Support a struggling family through an organization or church.

Deborah met Nancy, who had opened her home to those seeking help from SFFC and had a heart poised to serve. Nancy began asking Deborah about her pregnancy and what kinds of things her daughter enjoyed and liked to eat. It soon became apparent that Deborah had nothing ready for her new baby. Life circumstances had robbed her of the opportunity to joyfully prepare for and anticipate this addition to her family. Nancy began compiling a list of what Deborah might need, and Deborah began engaging in the conversation. The two were becoming friends.

When Deborah came out of the hospital, Nancy and her small group delivered two weeks' worth of meals. Her church provided clothing for the children, baby furniture, additional food, and even clothing for Deborah.

Deborah and her two daughters attend Nancy's church, and Deborah has been baptized. She wrote the agency to say thank you and that she had made friends and found a home.

Opening Your Heart

- Had you ever heard about how clear God's Word is on helping "the least of these" and who they are? If not, why do you think that is?

- Had you assumed caring for foster children, adopting, and perhaps making donations were the only ways to answer the call to care for vulnerable children? How has this chapter changed your thinking?

- If you see God's call to care more clearly than ever, do you also see it as a call more personal than ever? If so, how so?

- How will you commit to seeking God's leading as you consider your own call to care? Through prayer? Through study? Through conversation with others?

———— PRAYING FOR MY CALL ————

Father, it's so easy to not know, to forget, or even to ignore how clear your call is to care for the most vulnerable in our world. Help me embrace that call. Help me absorb it into my heart and mind and commit to discovering how you plan for me to humbly and uniquely answer. I want to serve you and make a difference. Amen.

2

Addressing Motivations

When we think we know how we're to personally answer the call to care, we must address our *why*—our motivations. Some motivations can be anything but healthy or helpful, and they can not only cause us to misinterpret how we can best answer the call to care, they can create expectations that adversely affect a child in life-changing ways. We'll talk about expectations in the next chapter, but let's first look at the risk of a call misunderstood.

A Call Misunderstood

Here's an account of how one couple thought they understood how they were to answer the call to care, but then struggled before learning how they could best serve.

Greg and Cassandra knew they were called to care, but as they moved through the paper work to become foster parents, they began to feel guilty about not being as excited about their fostering journey as the friends in their small group seemed to be about theirs.

Their first placement was difficult. The two young boys came with nothing, requiring a trip to buy basics such as pajamas, socks, underwear, and school clothes. Greg was out of town for the first few days, while Cassandra, who worked from home, struggled with caring for the kids and meeting her deadlines. She became frustrated and impatient, lashing out at Greg when he returned from work.

The boys were upset and angry. Their rage-filled outbursts were followed by periods of sobbing and clinging to each other and Cassandra. They were constantly in what their counselor called a state of fight-or-flight, hyperalert to any signs of danger. Cassandra found cookies, fruit, and even chewing gum hidden in their closet. Because they had experienced hunger so often, they felt they needed to ensure food would always be available.

It was not that Greg and Cassandra didn't love the boys; they did, and they cared for them well while these hurting children were in their home for two weeks. But they didn't have the sense of satisfaction they thought they'd have. They thought they should be excited about the next placement, and they felt guilty because they weren't.

They met with their foster care counselor to talk about how their first placement went. When they told her about their guilt and unhappiness, she asked them why they chose to foster. They admitted it had been at the prodding of their small group.

The counselor helped them see that the call to care doesn't always mean the call to foster or even adopt; there are other ways to care. Now Greg and Cassandra gladly provide meals for fostering friends, financially support Christian family services agencies, and pray daily for children in foster care. They're thrilled to know they're exactly where God wants them to be—caring for vulnerable children by helping those on the front lines.

Everyone who answers the call to care must determine if their motivations are leading them to a narrowly defined answer not meant for them. The motivation to help vulnerable children and families in a specific way can be based on anything from pure love to personal giftedness, from misplaced desires to a genuine desire to serve, from guilt to peer pressure.

Consider these three scenarios:

1. A couple was grieving their infertility, having experienced years of unsuccessful procedures and two miscarriages. They decided to adopt, because they thought a child would give them the family they wanted—and assuage their feelings of loss.
2. A family lost a child to illness, and they decided to adopt a child—to fill the hole in their hearts.
3. Several families in a couple's church prodded them to foster to adopt as they had. They already had several birth children, but they decided to foster a child—out of peer pressure and guilt.

To assuage their feelings of loss.
To fill the hole in their hearts.
Out of peer pressure and guilt.

These reasons could lead not only to disappointment and confusion for the parents, but to harmful expectations that adversely affect the children. We'll talk about damaging results in the next chapter.

Identifying Motivations

Identifying your call requires identifying your personal motives and scrutinizing them through self-examination, counseling, prayer, advice from experienced peers, and if you're considering foster care or adopting, brutal honesty about caring for children who have experienced hurt and loss. Ask yourself these types of questions:

Why is caring for children from hard places important to me?
If I decide to foster, how will I care for the children?
Do I want to foster in the interest of adoption? If so, why do I want to adopt?

Am I prepared to help children who have been traumatized, abused, neglected?

Am I ready to stay with this for the long term, knowing that healing usually takes time?

Why do I think my church should be involved in caring for children with special needs?

This couple understood their motivations and the call that was right for them.

Grace grew up in a quiet household, wishing for more buzz and excitement in her home. She told herself, *When I grow up, I want it to be lively!*

Fast-forward to when Grace and her husband, Ian, are parents of four daughters and ready for more. They attend an informational meeting at their church about a program in which children get temporary care in a family setting rather than entering the foster system.

Ian and Grace have hosted children several times, and Grace has the home she dreamed of when she was a child. When a placement is confirmed, they let their daughters know and they're all filled with excitement and anticipation as they wait for the children or child to arrive. The family takes the children to their church, where teachers, helpers, and friends make the children feel welcome.

These next three adoption stories show what can happen when individuals and families look carefully at their motivations and the family design they desire. Note the role prayer played in every case.

Bob and Helen, who married later in life, wanted several children. They went through the adoption process with the plan to adopt a sibling group of up to three children. When a call came about adopting four siblings, however, they believed they were the right match for them.

The siblings—two boys and two girls—came for a series of weekend visits, and then to stay. Although an adoption specialist supported them, as did their church and a counselor helping them with parenting skills, the first months were rough. Yet one significant factor kept their endurance and motivation strong.

"We prayed all the time," Bob said. Communication and prayer made the difference. They talked through everything in detail and then took it all to God in prayer, and this was their pattern throughout the adoption process.

• • •

Kirsten knew for sure that God had placed adoption on her heart. She and her husband, Mike, started praying about what that would look like for them and their two sons, and they felt led to start the process. When they received an email about a two-year-old girl who was struggling with being noticed in her foster family, they felt God speaking to them in a way they hadn't heard before, and they began the process to adopt her.

Alexis had never bonded with her mother and had sought attention from other places. But with time and patience she developed true attachment with Kirsten, Mike, and their boys.

• • •

After losing their newborn twin son, Gwen and Scott continued their work with an organization that cares for children in South Africa, while also caring for their three daughters. Later, they felt God was leading them toward adopting a child from that country. After prayer and thoughtful consideration to ensure their motivations were pure and their call was clear, they went forward with the plan to adopt.

They left open the gender, age, sibling number, and even medical condition. They eventually got a call about a little boy with medical needs. They thought they could not only manage his condition but help him thrive. Although they adopted out of birth order, he has developed an especially close relationship to his youngest sister, the one who lost her twin at birth. Watching them together, their mom said, is seeing a love story God created.

The Church and Motivations

For churches to come alongside families who care for vulnerable children means more than a one-time sermon and a welcome when the children arrive. This is a long-term commitment of support and a rewarding call to care. It's one thing for a church to talk about serving in this way; it's another thing completely to put that talk into action.

That's why churches also need to look at their motivations. They are strategically placed in communities to be beacons of hope and agents of change for vulnerable children and families, but pride and seeking power or prominence are unhelpful attitudes. For instance, is God truly leading the church, or are a couple of strong personalities putting themselves in charge?

It might be, too, that a church is called to care for its own vulnerable children before reaching out to those in the community, especially if children with physical, emotional, and mental challenges already in the church are marginalized or ignored. Church leaders are encouraged to first look hard at vulnerable people within their community and then look beyond their church family.

Here's a special caution for the church: Many church leaders do an excellent job of ensuring the people know they're called to care. However, many church *members* can be influenced by a secular society and its customs, beliefs, and values. Their motivations may make a difference in how the call to care is both assessed and carried out.

Read more about how churches can help keep families strong in chapter 16.

Pray, Seek, Search

Every individual, family, and church should prayerfully consider what are right and wrong motivations for taking part in the call to care. Good people can make wrong decisions if motivations aren't carefully considered. Good churches can be well-meaning but unintentionally create other issues if the motivations of individuals and groups are ignored.

Pray, seek good counsel, and search for the best way you can care for vulnerable children and families.

——— OPENING YOUR HEART ———

- How have you seen an unwise motivation drive someone to action? What was the result?
- How have you seen a wise motivation drive someone to action? What was the result?
- How do those examples translate to your understanding of identifying and evaluating motivations before answering the call to care?
- If you've discovered you're acting under a potentially problematic motivation, what help will you seek to address it?
- If you or your church is considering answering the call to care, have you identified your true motivations? If not, what will you do to start that process?

——— PRAYING FOR MY CALL ———

God, the last thing I want is to not hear you clearly as I try to answer your call to care. I want to be a blessing. Open my eyes and ears to not only receive your peace and guidance but also the guidance of others to help me determine my motivations before I take next steps. Amen.

3

Determining Expectations

Even when motivations are well-thought-out and wise, determining expectations and whether they're realistic is the next step. In this chapter we'll focus on the difference this exercise can make for parents considering bringing children into their homes. It's rarely enough to simply love a foster or adopted child.

Realistic expectations are gained through receiving counseling and talking to care experts and those who have had similar experiences. Remember these scenarios from the last chapter on motivations? The prospective adoptive or foster parents didn't understand their own motivations. That lack of understanding led to unrealistic expectations, setting up both adults and children for heartache.

- Grieving their long-time infertility, a couple adopted because they thought a child would assuage their feelings of loss. That child, however, no matter how hard he tried, never could meet their expectation to be the "perfect" child they'd always wanted—and he knew it.

- A couple decided to adopt to fill the hole left in their hearts when they lost a child to illness. But that child couldn't change their need to grieve the loss of their daughter and could never replace her.
- A couple with several biological children decided to foster to adopt out of guilt and peer pressure. Shy, with a history of neglect and dealing with the loss of all he'd known, the boy sensed his new parents' disappointment in how he didn't fit in with the family. He was treated differently— sometimes separately—from the other children, and he became withdrawn, making the placement even more difficult.

Even if you are loving your child as well as you can, adopted children fear that they don't belong to their new family and may incorrectly perceive certain parental behaviors as rejection.

Following are some families' experiences that help illustrate how crucial realistic expectations are. The cautionary stories are meant to encourage and educate, not to discourage. Only a small percentage of adoptions are disrupted, and a high percentage of foster placements are successful.

Expectations Gone Awry

The Smith family seemed to have the right motivations behind their desire to adopt a child through the foster care system. They loved God, they loved children, and they wanted to help a child who needed a home. They completed the process to become foster parents and welcomed the first placement, which was of a ten-year-old boy we'll call Kevin.

Kevin stayed with them for fourteen months before the court declared him available for adoption. After many attempts to have his birth parents follow the treatment plan meant to correct their neglectful behavior, the court had terminated their parental rights. The Smiths were thrilled and immediately began the process of adopting him. They thought he would be excited to join their other three children, ages eight, eleven, and thirteen, in a forever family. When he asked about his mom, his foster parents told him he was going to be part of their family now.

But they were taken aback by the question. It didn't occur to them that Kevin might be grieved by the loss of his mother or because his mom couldn't care for him and provide a safe home. They never thought about his need to mourn the loss of his first family. They expected immediate excitement about finding a forever home far away from the drama and pain in his previous life. But children who experience neglect and abuse still love their parents and often blame themselves when they are removed from their parents' care.

Kevin began to withdraw from them and had angry outbursts, screamed, and hit people. He began bed-wetting and getting into trouble at school. It wasn't long before the family withdrew their adoption petition, sad and upset that the boy didn't seem to want what they offered him. He rejoined the foster system, and they decided against continuing as foster parents.

The Smiths weren't wrong in wanting to help a child who needed a family. They were mistaken, however, to expect Kevin to be as excited about their plans as they were. At age ten, he had experienced considerable trauma, including being removed from his home, watching his father be arrested and later jailed, and seeing his mother succumb to drug and alcohol addiction, resulting in her neglecting him. A child's thoughts can go like this: *If my parents couldn't keep me, how can I trust another family to keep me forever?*

Kevin needed time, space, support, and, most of all, understanding to help him process everything he'd experienced. While he enjoyed the foster family he'd been living with, when they told him they wanted to adopt him, fear and anxiety overwhelmed him. He missed his mom; adoption made it real that he would never live with her again. Although social workers had looked for family members able to care for him over those fourteen months, they'd found none. Yet Kevin still didn't understand why his grandparents or another relative didn't adopt him.

On some level Kevin feared he was the one responsible for having to leave his mom in the first place, and he feared he might not be good enough for this new family either.

His foster family expected him to be grateful for this change, jump immediately into their family life, and begin doing better in school. These expectations were never expressed in words, but later it became clear to them that they had been expecting more than reality provided. Children who come from hard places of abuse and neglect are still attached to their parents and other family, often blaming themselves for what went wrong in the adults' lives.

Expectations Managed Well

David and Ivy, who had started the adoption process, got a call about a child born prematurely in another part of their state whose mother was creating an adoption plan.

The baby's two older siblings had cystic fibrosis, and she was undergoing tests to determine if she had it as well. Would they be willing to adopt a child with possible special needs? Yes, they decided after careful consideration. They would.

The mother chose them as the parents for her newborn daughter, and David and Ivy began making the two-hundred-mile round trip to visit the baby, named Caroline, several times a week. These adoptive parents knew bonding with this baby was important to her growth and healing, and they also knew she may very well have medical challenges.

Their expectations were grounded in an understanding of what the future might hold; they knew medical care might be necessary and that developmental delays and the need for a lifetime of care were possible, but they felt they were ready.

David and Ivy brought Caroline home just a few months after her birth, and a few months later they became her parents. Today

Caroline shows no sign of cystic fibrosis, although she has challenges related to her premature birth, and is happy and healthy, but that doesn't change the fact that the couple carefully examined their expectations and were prepared for a different outcome.

When a sixteen-year-old mother gave birth to her son prematurely and asked for agency help, Luis and Camila were chosen to be Samuel's adoptive parents. They met him in a temporary placement before taking him home as foster parents with intent to adopt.

Samuel lost weight and didn't gain it back as newborns typically do. After weeks of tests and hospitalizations, he was diagnosed with Septo-optic dysplasia. He would have vision, pituitary, and cognition challenges.

As required, the agency informed Luis and Camila they weren't obligated to adopt Samuel. But the couple had begun to bond with him, and they chose to learn what to expect, so their expectations were realistic. As they prayed about the future, they felt God say, *Just as you would accept a biological child, accept this child I've given to you.*

At eleven, Samuel is vision impaired but not blind, and he can walk and has some verbal skills. His sisters adore him. "He's doing great," his mom said. "He's a happy guy."

How to Manage Expectations

Managing expectations for everyone involved can be broken into three major categories: training, solidarity, and understanding.

1. Training: Learning What You Don't Know

Whether you're considering parenting an adopted or foster child (or volunteering in the call to care in some other way), receiving training to know what to expect is crucial for successfully determining and managing expectations. Also, you need knowledge on how to nurture your child and respond to their special needs. (More information about training is found in the next chapter.)

2. Solidarity: Standing Together

At times fathers do not understand the important role they play for the child and their spouse. Both parents in a family must be fully involved and committed to the call to care for vulnerable children in their home. If that expectation is overlooked, couples and families can face trouble from the start. All children are capable of pitting one parent against another; throw in a wounded, traumatized child just trying to survive, and the problems can magnify. Also, when parents know they can count on each other for emotional support, spiritual strength, and childcare when a good nap is needed, outcomes for the child improve. When a single person adopts, those in their support system must be committed to not only being educated but to staying engaged.

Another group with expectations is the extended family. Will grandparents, aunts, uncles—even friends—readily accept a child with disabilities, a child from another culture or race, or a foster child from another part of the city? One grandmother was heard to say, "These are my three birth grandchildren, and this is my adopted grandchild." Singling out that child can lead to feelings of being different and "not enough," which affects the family relationships and sense of trust.

And have you seen large parties at airports—happy friends and relatives with balloons, waving signs, waiting to greet a family arriving home with a newly adopted child from overseas? It is a great idea, but the reality is that the parents are exhausted and the child is frightened by the unfamiliar faces, new surroundings, and noise. Solidarity can mean knowing when to give a newly formed family some space. So keep these welcome-home greetings short.

3. Understanding: Putting Knowledge to Use

The last component is simply using what you've learned to understand. All the knowledge and solidarity in the world won't be enough if you don't use it to understand expectations and how to address them. Here are some ways you can do that.

Make assessments, not assumptions. In the United States, state child welfare departments usually have systems to help set realistic expectations for foster parents.

A child who is assessed to have higher needs and challenges will likely require more care, intervention services, and other therapies. The assessment system varies by state, but it's vital to helping foster parents manage their expectations.

One family was fostering two young teenagers who had experienced poverty and a lack of some of the basic things that every child needs. The foster mom took them to a clothing store her kids liked, thinking these kids would too. But they didn't.

"My expectation was that they would value what my kids valued," she said.

The teenagers instead liked clothes from large discount stores where they were used to shopping and where their friends and peers had shopped and could afford. The foster mom had to reevaluate her expectations regarding the likes and dislikes of the teens in her care.

By the way, when we bring children into a home, our desire to provide and make them happy can motivate us to give them video games, top-of-the-line clothing, and a gorgeous room. What they might really want is a safe place to sleep, food they're used to, and help figuring out a new culture or language. Our desire to help and show our love can sometimes overwhelm. Sensitivity and awareness are key.

Realize some expectations are subtle. Not all expectations can be determined ahead of time. If, for instance, a couple is musically inclined, they might assume without even realizing it that an adopted child will love music too. The seemingly healthy child may be found to have hearing problems that weren't known at the time of adoption, surprising the adoptive parents who assumed she'd be healthy (though even birth parents cannot assume health for a biological child). Another area for managing expectations is academic achievement. Due to a history of neglect, many children will require assistance with homework, and they may struggle in their education.

Understand and prepare for challenging behaviors. If parents expect tantrums, defiance, hoarding, challenges with attaching, or fighting from the children in their care, they aren't surprised when it happens and understand why it's happening. It doesn't always make it easier to deal with, but that understanding adds a layer of compassion.

Teenagers with trauma in their past may not have moved past their trauma age (age at which the events occurred), using the behavior of a much younger child as a form of expression. All two-year-olds present challenges, but expectations for a two-year-old who has had a troubling life might need adjustment.

Two-year-old Ellie was the oldest of three siblings, all born a year apart and living in the same foster home. Her birth mother had been emotionally absent, and, as a result, the lack of secure attachment caused her to seek attention wherever she could find it. She initiated hugs and conversations with strangers and didn't understand appropriate boundaries. Her constant battle to be noticed was becoming increasingly challenging for her foster parents, but with her younger sisters also in their care, it was difficult for them to give her the one-on-one attention important for her to thrive.

When potential adoptive parents Jake and Lucie received an email about Ellie, they also learned what to expect from her and what she needed. When she came into their home, she appeared to attach quickly to the family, but it was an insecure attachment. The road to secure attachment was long and hard, and along the way, whenever Ellie was angry or upset, she focused her rage on Lucie. Despite the challenges, though, it was clear Ellie was a good fit as the only girl and youngest child.

Apply What You Learn about Attachment

Children need to attach to the nuclear family first, and with effective communication, other family members will accept that and provide the space needed for them to attach. Education can go a long way toward helping extended family and even neighbors, church workers, and school employees manage their expectations regarding the new child in a home.

Attachment styles and history are as important to the new parents as they are to the children. Adults are encouraged to work through their own attachment issues, so they can find success in what's been called "the dance of attachment."[1] A new adoptive father whose own father was distant and angry may find attaching to the new child difficult. A foster mom who communicates love through physical touch may be distressed when a child with autism or who has experienced abuse recoils from her touch.

Every child is looking for a trusting relationship, despite any impairments or other issues. They may have hurts and emotional scars making it harder for them to trust at a level that leads to attachment. And they'll test foster parents, because many kids would rather give those adults a reason to reject them—their behavior—than be rejected again for no fault of their own.

This story illustrates how we can also learn from expectations we discover aren't necessarily valid.

Shortly after completing their foster care training and paper work, Charles and Rolanda received a call saying a child needed immediate placement that day. Rolanda was soon holding the eighteen-month-old boy who would become their son, and the adoption was fourteen months later.

"I took a little longer to really feel warmly toward him than I expected," she said. "I thought there was something wrong with me."

When she joined a group of adoptive mothers and learned about some of their experiences, however, she realized her idea of instant love had been a myth and her expectation had not been necessarily realistic.

Yes, misplaced expectations can cause everything from confusion and struggle to heartache and long-term damage, but determining expectations, embracing realistic expectations, and managing expectations can bring children and families together.

43

———— OPENING YOUR HEART ————

- Have you learned to determine and manage your expectations in a new situation? How?

- Have you ever realized you had an expectation that wasn't valid? What was it? How did you modify what you originally thought?

- If you're considering adoption or foster care, what expectations do you have? Do you expect a child to be grateful? Bond immediately? Instantly love you? What expectations might your extended family members have? How can you help manage those expectations?

- What agencies or organizations might you turn to for training?

- If your church is or is thinking about helping children from hard places, what do you think are its expectations? How can you help manage those expectations?

- If you have other children, have you considered how they will be affected if you foster or adopt? Some parents feel guilty because they need to spend extra time with the adopted or foster child and have less time for their other children.

———— PRAYING FOR MY CALL ————

Lord, we all have expectations, and sometimes we don't even realize we have them. Help me identify, evaluate, and address the expectations I have and amend them as necessary, so I can realistically and effectively answer the call to care you have for me. I want my expectations to align with yours. Amen.

4

Assessing Preparedness

Once you pray about what answering the call to care looks like for you and examine your motives and expectations, it's important to practically assess your preparedness. Rushing full speed ahead without a plan, patience, and a good dose of reality can be a recipe for disaster, with children's hearts on the line.

To avoid disappointment, stress, and burnout, as well as to ensure your response to the call to care is best suited to your circumstances and needs, think through the practical side of the call you're pursuing. Professional adoption or placement staff can help you work through all these areas, but here are three you can start thinking about now.

1. Your Family Life

If you already have children, have you considered how adding another child or more children might impact your family and extended family? Maybe they, especially your children, have reservations they're hesitant to share.

If you're considering foster care, a temporary care program, or refugee care, will the other souls in your care be able to handle well the constant coming and going of kids? Some family members may be concerned about becoming too attached to a child and having a tough time letting go. Others might fear they won't want to bond with the children at all because they'll probably be gone soon.

Think also about the impact the constant caring for those in need, and especially those with special needs, could put on your spouse and your marriage, even if you have a strong relationship.

2. The Children You'll Care For

You care for people best when you're as prepared as you can be for how they might behave or how they might react in response to you. Children brought into your home might suffer from sleeplessness or sensory meltdowns (a reaction to too much sensory input). They might exhibit grief or loneliness or anger. They might wet the bed, sleep poorly, or hoard food.

3. Your Schedule and Resources

Schedules and resources can become overburdened with the additional transportation, health care, emotional care, and education needs of children who have experienced abuse, neglect, abandonment, or other trauma. What will it look like to add this kind of strain to your household, either permanently or temporarily? Consider these scenarios:

- Alan and Kate want to help refugees resettle in their area, but their teenage children's sporting events sometimes take up nearly every weeknight as well as Saturdays. Sundays mean church responsibilities and preparing for the week. How can they fit the needs of a refugee family into their packed schedule?

- Morgan feels the call to participate in the foster care network, but he works third shift. His family lives far away, and his friends are working or caring for their families. If he welcomes a child into his home, who would provide care while he works and sleeps?
- Jude and Mia feel the call to adopt, but they're both working full-time to pay off a mountain of school loan debt. They have no money to spare.
- Gabrielle loves the idea of hosting a child through Safe Families for Children, but she works full-time in a fast-paced and hectic job she loves, with almost no room for sick days or unexpected time off. The two days or two weeks with children in her home would be difficult to manage.
- Jayson would like to travel overseas to assist with family-based care support, but money is tight and vacation time is precious because he's used a lot of it to help care for his elderly parents.

Room in your heart doesn't necessarily mean room in your life. The adage "God will provide" is heard many times from people eager to care for children and families. God provides many things at many times, yes, but his plans include good and realistic planning on our part.

How to Assess Realities and Prepare

It's not enough to acknowledge the need to face realties and prepare; you must be willing to slow down and follow through.

Take the Time to Learn

Classes from qualified agencies are good places to receive eye-opening and realistic assessment and preparedness. As mentioned before, training is one key component of determining and

---

Bethany Christian Services Training

Bethany, for example, offers training—required for those who will care for children—and counseling services for a wide range of needs. Potential foster and adoptive parents and Safe Families for Children host families take classes and can receive counseling help and on-call help as needed. Pregnancy and adoption planning is offered for parents considering creating an adoption plan. Those interested in refugee work can receive training to help them understand the issues involved in relocation. All of this is part of helping families and individuals prepare to welcome vulnerable children and families into their homes and hearts.

---

managing expectations, but it can also prepare you to respond to God's call in all sorts of practical ways.

Talking to those ahead of you on the path helps, as do receiving counseling, talking with caseworkers and support groups, and reading up on the topic, such as reading this book and information your agency makes available. (See the back of this book for a list of recommended books for adoptive and foster care parents.)

Make and Use Lists

Nothing can fully prepare you for stepping into the trenches of day-to-day life with a child or family in crisis. But making and using a list of practical considerations can help. Your list depends on how God has called you to serve, but here are sample starter checklists that can help you as you consider adoption and foster care, refugee care, or traveling overseas.

ADOPTION AND FOSTER CARE

- health care (appointments, surgeries, treatments, therapy)
- trauma histories

- bedroom realignment and furnishings
- food allergies, sensitivities, and preferences
- environmental allergies
- transportation
- educational needs (transportation, tutoring, accommodation for learning challenges)
- childcare

REFUGEE CARE

- language differences
- food preferences
- traumatic history
- extended family issues
- cultural differences regarding family dynamics, work, raising children
- job needs, skills, and preferences
- housing
- household goods and furnishings
- education needs
- transportation
- legal services/citizenship

TRAVELING OVERSEAS

- valid passport and visa
- immunizations and medications
- general physical health
- funds for tickets and travel needs
- clothing needs for expected weather and temperatures
- in-country assistance upon arrival
- translation needs

- cultural differences
- appropriate gift giving

Here's how one couple prepared for their call to foster vulnerable children:

Caleb and Rae had talked about fostering children even before Rae felt especially led after attending a conference about orphans and vulnerable children. When she returned home, she told Caleb about it, and he was interested. After further consideration, prayer, and discussion with their extended family and young children, they started the process of preparation.

First, they learned about the avenues available in their community to become licensed for foster care. When they chose an agency, they signed up for all the training and classes necessary and faithfully attended. They also took care of the requirements for their home, such as locking away or adequately guarding things like medicines and household cleaning products; installing the kinds of gates necessary for stairs; and preparing adequate beds and bedroom arrangements. They also designated how many children, and at what ages, they could accommodate at one time, given they had two biological children and a van with room for a limited number of car seats, which they also obtained.

When they received their license and first placement, they were as ready as possible so they could concentrate on the love and care their foster children needed from them.

Preparedness for Churches

Your church wants to begin welcoming families with children with special needs, host support groups for adoptive and foster care families, or sponsor a refugee family. The church building was built before handicapped accessibility was required, no families who attend have a child with special needs, and no research has been done on refugee sponsorship.

A preparedness assessment is a must. For a checklist to begin that work and many other helps for the church poised to answer the call to care, see chapter 16.

Sometimes, though, a church answers the call to care beginning with one significant, simple, successful project.

The Bethany Christian Services branch in a large city holds a diaper drive once a month and gives away as many as sixteen thousand diapers to local families in need. The mission ministry in one church, ready to take part, decided to involve the whole congregation, but they had to get the word out. That took some preparation.

First, they set up a collection box in the common area of their building. Then they spread the word through their weekly email blasts, monthly newsletter, and social media. The church had a preschool, and the director spread the word to those families as well.

The people of the church and families of the preschool responded, but participation didn't end there. When the church's vacation Bible school team chose the diaper drive as their mission for the week, 2,400 diapers and seventy-five packs of wipes were donated.

Church leadership also prepared to help with this monthly drive on an ongoing basis. The congregation knows the drive continues every month, and mission team members monitor the collection box at the church. When it's full they deliver the items to Bethany's office.

The church realizes they can't help everyone in need, but as they sought to lead their people to love, bless, and serve others in Jesus' name, they found and prepared well for this simple but meaningful way both adults and children could reach out to their community.

—— OPENING YOUR HEART ——

- Take a careful look at your family, your resources, and any assumptions you've made without determining what's realistic. Is your family truly on board with the idea of foster care or adoption?

- Do you have margin in your schedule to welcome others into your life? Do you have a financial plan in place to support the call you hear?
- Have you considered how you will prepare for refugee care, foster care, or adoption—mentally, emotionally, practically? What counseling will you need or have you received?
- Who will be your support system to give you an emotional or practical boost when you need it?
- How can you help others prepare to care for vulnerable children or families? What resources do you have to share to make their loads lighter?
- What would you add to the checklists in this chapter?

--------- PRAYING FOR MY CALL ---------

Father, it's easy to get excited about a new way to serve and rush ahead without prayer and adequate planning and preparation. If necessary, slow me down. Show me not only how you want me to serve but also all the ways I need to prepare. Then give me the guidance, confidence, and wisdom I need to follow through. Amen.

PART TWO

EXPLORING FOSTER CARE AND ADOPTION

5

A Close Look at Foster Care

The first goal of child welfare authorities is to keep a child in their family. The next best choice is to keep the child with relatives or kin. Keeping a child in a family with genetic connections and history reduces his or her experience of loss and disruption, which can have long-term implications. Many organizations and programs help facilitate this type of family preservation.

But when that's not possible, foster care and adoption can come into play. Those are the options we'll consider in this part of the book, and we'll begin with a close look at foster care.

In all honesty, foster care can be the most difficult interpretation of the call to care for vulnerable children. But foster care is also one of the most rewarding interpretations. A foster home can be a picture of a stable, functioning family to children who may have never seen one before. Foster parents can give them the love and security they need and crave.

Here's one woman's foster care story:

Opal and her husband, Nick, are called to provide foster care to children. In their large city alone, over six thousand kids are in care, and the two of them have fostered nearly twenty children over the years.

Opal encourages others to consider fostering as well. Sometimes they're concerned about how fostering will affect the children in the home, but she says her own boys have learned a lot about being patient and caring for people who aren't able to care for themselves. More often she hears concerns about how to handle parting with a foster child.

"I turn that back to them and say, 'What will happen to this child if he or she isn't in an environment where they learn that they are precious and loved? Consider serving just one child at a time, and you can make an impact.'

"I get to be the vehicle of change for one precious child," she said. "I get to help someone who needs a home."

Foster parenting, however, does require remarkable levels of flexibility and resilience, because, like every answer to the call to care, fostering comes with costs.

Emotional Cost

One of the greatest tensions for foster parents is giving all of themselves to children when they know they probably won't be with them forever. Foster care agencies often hear potential foster parents say they're concerned they won't be able to handle saying good-bye.

Let's not downplay those feelings. The grief can indeed be intense as foster parents let go of children they've come to love. After all, they've been caring for them day after day, helping them work through the trauma they've experienced, and they've seen the progress they've made. A child in a foster home also might not be capable of returning love. But foster parents walling off emotions to protect themselves isn't what children in foster care need. They need all the love foster parents can give.

Not to discourage those who feel the call to foster, but foster parents indeed face an emotional journey. Almost all children who come into foster care have been removed from homes under circumstances where their safety was threatened by abuse or neglect.

These kids are emotionally wounded and struggle with a variety of issues because of that wounding.

Time Cost

Consider this list—more detailed than the checklist for foster care and adoption in the last chapter—of what foster parents may face as care providers for children who have become wards of the state because of abuse or neglect, or during interims before the permanency of adoption.

- Doctor visits for well-baby checks, vaccinations, illnesses, and physicals
- Specialist visits for a child with physical disabilities or medical needs
- Visits to counselors, psychiatrists, and psychologists
- Transportation to and from school, preschool, sports, and/or after-school programs
- Meetings with school officials and teachers and being the child's advocate for needed supportive services or testing
- Assistance with homework (many children have fallen behind in grade level)
- Transportation to supervised visits with birth parents and/ or siblings
- Court appearances
- Extra time to care for a child's feelings of loss and grief and to correct acting out

Questions Everyone Should Ask

Here are some of the questions everyone should ask before they embark on the foster parent journey.

Is my immediate family committed to providing this kind of care? You may not know the challenges ahead, but are you and your family ready to work through them? If your spouse or children are not on board, resentment and anger can arise. Family members may sabotage relationships with foster children, withdraw, or act out, putting even more strain on a new relationship. Some foster moms have initially felt guilty for giving more time to their foster child than to their other children.

Extended family should also be made aware of plans, so they'll not be surprised if you show up to family parties with another child in tow. They need to know they'll need help learning how to be helpful and supportive of the child, understanding attachment challenges for a child hurt by those who were supposed to love and protect him, and, if necessary, knowing how to help with childcare needs if they are willing, especially if licensing requirements come into play.

Is my home equipped for additional children? This may seem a little persnickety, but let's face it: Your teenage daughter won't want to share a room with a rambunctious three-year-old. You shouldn't move your son to a dark and dank basement to make room for a foster child.

Do you have room for children to play? Can stairs be blocked off to prevent tumbles? Is your yard fenced if you live on a busy street? Do you have enough beds and dressers? Enough bathrooms? Do you know what requirements pertain to your home before you can be licensed for foster care?

Do I have adequate transportation? Do you have a vehicle always available for taking foster children to a variety of appointments, church, family events, and school? Is it big enough to hold both your children and foster children? Do you have appropriate car seats?

What does my support system look like? Do you have family in the area who can help with childcare and transportation if needed? Do you have friends you can rely on for help and advice? What about daycare if you work outside the home? Do you have a pastor or other clergy member you can talk to and who will pray for you? Do they understand the challenges that kids face when in foster care and that your family is now facing?

Do I have a good understanding of what to expect? Do you understand the state of the children coming into your home? What do you know about the impact of trauma and how it comes out in behavior? Do you know how to address tantrums and other acting-out behaviors? Are you ready to care for a newborn?

Potential foster parents must go through a screening process, have a home study, and meet state licensing standards—all of which can take at least six months. This process will help you think through the questions above. Parents also participate in training sessions, so they'll know what to expect and how to handle challenging behaviors and other issues that might arise.

The story of the good Samaritan in the Bible has an interesting point that applies to foster parenting. The Samaritan helped the wounded Jewish man without expectation of reward or honor. He just helped him with kindness and competence. We have no record of whether the injured man repaid him in any way.

Foster parents, too, must come into the program not expecting adulation and thanks, especially from the vulnerable children they care for. It's easy to expect the kids to be grateful and behave, but they are traumatized children dealing with feelings and events they not only don't understand, but that have changed the way they react to the world. Foster parents must love them—and love them without expectations.

This area of care for vulnerable children can be emotionally draining, stressful, and disappointing—and plain old hard work. But it's the perfect opportunity to step up and live out the biblical mandate to care for the world's most vulnerable. It was for this couple, who got a welcome, though challenging, surprise.

Denise and Paul completed their home study and were licensed to provide foster care for children of all ages. Two weeks later, they received a call at eleven thirty at night. Could they take two boys ages four and six that night? They agreed, and an hour later they heard a knock on the door. They'd just finished making up the boys' beds.

There stood a social worker and two frightened children who had just watched their mom being driven off in a police cruiser as they sat in the social worker's car. They were wearing Spiderman pajamas, and each gripped a stuffed animal given to him by that social worker. They had nothing else.

These brand-new foster parents looked as much like deer in the headlights as the children. But they welcomed them warmly and offered them snacks. Soon the exhausted boys were settled into bed, and Denise and Paul sat looking at each other, grinning. They were finally foster parents.

But they were foster parents without a stitch of clothing for the boys, no idea what they liked to eat, and no clue what they liked to play with or whether to take them to school the next day. The next morning, however, a nonprofit dedicated to helping vulnerable children dropped off a backpack filled with underwear and socks, two outfits, two toothbrushes, and a few small toys for each boy.

Their foster care journey had begun.

Kids Aging Out of the System

This book would be remiss if it didn't note the trends for kids in foster care who age out at eighteen without a support system. As the website for the Christian Alliance for Orphans states, "As older orphans and foster children age out of care, the trends are heartbreaking: homelessness, substance abuse, trafficking, crime and incarceration await many who lack adequate support networks."[1]

That's what makes the following story so significant—and sure to touch any heart.

Nearly twenty years ago, Simon was seventeen and about to age out of the foster care system. He'd lived with his alcoholic mother until he was twelve, and then he bounced from home to home for years. During his senior year of high school, he spent most of his nights with friends after his relationship with his foster mother deteriorated, but his social worker told him he needed a designated place to stay.

Foster Care Overseas

In Africa, there is a strong sense of family cohesiveness, but not an overall realization of the family's critical role in caring for children. That role has become clearer as families have disintegrated due to poverty, HIV, and other factors.

Bethany's foster-to-adopt concept introduced a cultural shift in the approach to child welfare. The concept of an African family caring for a biological child is deeply entrenched, but the idea of caring for a child not biologically part of your family is entirely new. It requires a profound understanding and conviction about why you would do this. . . .

From our faith perspective, we believe God's design is for every child, everywhere, to have a loving family. Through local African churches, families are beginning to see that every child is our responsibility, in an orphanage or on the streets. When we started the foster-to-adopt program in Ethiopia, many thought our biggest challenge would be finding enough families for all the children who needed homes. But to our surprise, the opposite happened. In my local community, where there was once no Amharic word for foster care, we found more families willing to be trained as foster parents than we had waiting children. When we present this opportunity in local churches, people say, "I've wanted to do this for a long time. God has used you to bring this message."[2]

—Sebilu Bodja, director of Africa operations

Enter Tim and Melissa, who had a three-and-a-half-year-old and were expecting another child. They were only a decade older than Simon, but they had become aware of his need and they wanted to act as his foster parents. He soon moved in.

This was the first time Simon had ever received unconditional love and support. When Melissa gave him a house key, he kept returning it every time he used it. It took him a while to realize she meant for him to keep it.

Simon unexpectedly received a scholarship to play baseball in college, but he had already enlisted in the army. Tim went to the recruiting office, dressed in a suit and carrying a briefcase to look as official as possible, to convince them to release Simon from service. It worked.

Simon played baseball all through college and today is a bank executive. He and his wife have four children, and he serves on his local Bethany Christian Services board.

"I saw the face of Christ through Tim and Melissa," he said. "I never imagined where I'd be today without them."

OPENING YOUR HEART

- How has reading this chapter opened your heart to consider foster care or to support those who foster?
- If you put yourself in the place of foster parents, what do you think or feel? What help do you think they most need?
- What are your biggest concerns or fears about foster care? If you're considering fostering, write down those concerns and fears, and then talk to a foster care specialist.
- Have an honest discussion with your family to hear what they have to say about fostering.
- How might your church offer support for foster parents?

PRAYING FOR MY CALL

God, foster care isn't for the faint of heart, but I see how it's a part of your call to care and that it can have rewards beyond what we can measure. Children's hearts are on the line. Help me to discern if the needs in foster care are where you want me to answer your call and how you want me to do so. Amen.

6

A Close Look at Adoption

Adoption has many faces—each one a beautiful picture of how children in need are welcomed into forever families. Some join new families because their birth parents, for one or more of a myriad of reasons, are unable to parent, at least at that point in time. Others are in need of new families because of abuse or neglect by their birth parents, and still others are orphaned and vulnerable because of poverty, abandonment, or death. We'll talk about intercountry adoption in a later chapter, but many children overseas are orphaned because of war or violence.

Types of Adoption

Knowing the types of adoption is helpful to anyone who is considering this call to care, who knows a child who needs a home, or who feels called to support adoption.

- **Domestic adoption:** adoption of a child or children born in the United States
- **Intercountry (or international) adoption:** adoption of a child or children born outside the United States

- **Infant adoption:** adoption of a child from birth to age two, approximately
- **Older child adoption:** adoption of any child no longer considered an infant
- **Foster care adoption:** adoption of a child who is in the foster care system and is available for adoption because the rights of their birth parents have been terminated by the court
- **Relative adoption:** adoption by a relative of the child
- **Stepparent adoption:** adoption by a stepparent after marriage to child's parent

It's important to note that when a child is adopted in the United States, no matter how, he or she becomes a member of the family. No legal difference exists between birth children and adopted children, nor is there any legal question about who the child's parents are, although children usually, and should always, know they have both biological and adoptive parents.

Adoption Statistics for the United States

In the United States in 2014, 18,329 infants were adopted[1] (private domestic adoptions are not tracked separately from other kinds of adoption at this time). Intercountry adoptions have been decreasing since 2004; the latest available number is 4,174 for 2017.[2] The United States Children's Bureau reported that in 2017, 59,430 children were adopted from the US foster care system, with the number of waiting children at 123,437.[3]

Semi-open and Open Adoptions

Adoption used to mean severing all ties between the child and the birth parents, birth family, and even birth culture. Open adoption was first introduced in domestic infant adoption in the 1970s. Once a trend, it's now much more the norm. Children adopted out of foster care often know about their birth families, even if official ties have been severed. Even intercountry adoptions, due in part to social media and other factors, have far more openness. The idea that adoptees or adoptive families will never know of or have contact with birth families is of the past, as social media platforms and internet searches reshape ideas of anonymity.

Open adoption has been described by the levels of information shared and the amount of planned contact with the birth parents. What we have found is that, like other relationships, the amount of contact can vary with time, and what is more important is the depth and strength of the relationship. As we think about the relationships between birth families, adoptive families, and adoptees, we prefer the term relational adoption to encompass the trust and caring necessary to ongoing connection.

The openness also comes from a new understanding of the damage and pain an adoption plan can cause for birth parents. The choice to relinquish a child is never easy and will always be a loss that changes the parents forever. The Donaldson Adoption Institute tells us birth parents can mourn the loss even while acknowledging they've made the best choice for the child.[4] Having contact with the birth family can help the healing, though it doesn't lessen the loss.

Professional counselors and adoptive parents can help.

Erin was twenty-five, had a five-year-old son, and had had an abortion at age eighteen. When she found she was pregnant after a one-night stand, she considered abortion again, but she knew it would devastate her.

With help from a pregnancy counselor, she began to plan for an open adoption. She got to know Kelly and John, who already had an adopted child who was biracial, just like Erin's child would be. Kelly was there for the baby's birth, and Erin was able to watch his dedication at church via Skype.

"I am at peace," Erin said at seven weeks post-birth, though she still grieved not being with her child daily. "I'm so very comfortable with Kelly and John, I trust them, and I will always be part of my son's life."

Adoptees have also been heard, saying loud and clear that they need and deserve to know their histories and their stories. When secrecy shrouded adoption and the prevailing belief was that adoptive families were more important than biological history, only de-identified social medical histories were available. Now as more is learned about the importance of genetic history and early experiences, more detailed social and medical information is gathered and shared, and the role of continually updating that information is recognized. Once-closed adoptions from years past are also opening as adoptees search for birth parents and family. Many adults who didn't have any information on their birth families are now using old records and social media to find their families of origin.

The historic 1973 US Supreme Court Roe v. Wade decision declaring that abortion is a constitutional right also played a role in the adoption landscape. As more women had access to legal abortion services for unintended pregnancies, fewer children became available for adoption. But when mothers did decide on adoption, they had a much greater say in their adoption plans, and many wanted to know who would raise their children.

Adoption Poses Unique Relational Considerations

We have covered motivations and expectations for pursuing the call to care, but here are some relational considerations specific to adoption:

For the Birth Parents

- Is someone pushing the parents to release their child for adoption? For a woman, is her boyfriend or husband pushing her to release her child for adoption?
- Who will be a support to the birth family in their loss and grief?

- Does an expectant mother want to parent her child, but she's afraid because she doesn't have the support she'll need?

For the Adoptive Parents

- Are prospective adoptive parents able to embrace the birth family and the child's birth history?
- Is an element of secrecy at play? Some couples want to keep their infertility issues hidden—especially from people who think having biological children is a sign of God's favor. They may not want anyone to know they're adopting for any number of reasons—pride, inheritance issues, or even fear of the child being taken away.

These issues and others like them are best addressed before or at least early in the adoption process. A pastor, counselor, or adoption specialist can help assess complicated issues and feelings before a child is brought into a home.

Adoption Is Not One-Size-Fits-All

Always, the bottom line is the safety and care of children, but adoption is as varied as the families and children involved. For instance, we tend to think of adoption as involving only non-relatives, but many adoptions involve extended family members who step up to care for children in need of love and forever homes.

This story illustrates that possibility.

Cynthia and Kyle's teenage niece fell under the influence of a controlling boyfriend, alcohol, and, later, drugs. When they learned of her pregnancy, they contacted her to offer what help they could. It was clear she couldn't and didn't want to parent. Might these parents of three children be open to adoption? They wondered and prayed, asking God to open the door in an obvious way.

They didn't have long to wait. Their niece approached them about adopting the baby. Her parents were divorced, and both had busy careers. Her grandparents were too old to care for an infant. The child's father was interested in parenting but felt that he would not have the stability or support that he would need, especially with his own work at recovery.

Cynthia and Kyle asked their children what they thought, sought advice from close friends and an adoption counselor, and talked with their niece. She asked again, and they agreed to adopt her daughter.

A child who could have been aborted or faced a life of chaos and turmoil instead gained a loving, supportive family.

Olympic gymnast Simone Biles raised awareness of family adoption when she was pressed by a reporter about her adoption by her grandparents Ron and Nellie Biles. "They may be mom and dad but they are NOT her parents," the reporter wrote in a now-deleted tweet.[5] His comments brought the adoption and gymnastics communities to arms. Many tweeted in response that the couple are Simone and her sister's parents regardless of how they came to the role.

Biles has been open about how her family came together, but the controversy highlights misconceptions and ignorance about what adoption means.

Here are three more stories highlighting adoption. No two adoptions are the same; don't expect that. But see what you can learn and embrace from each of these accounts.

Gillian and Ben always thought adoption was a way for them to fulfill their dream of becoming parents. "I hadn't thought about it from the birth mother's perspective," Gillian said.

They had completed the paper work when they got a call about an expectant mom forming an adoption plan. Crystal was living with her aunt and uncle in San Diego while pregnant, and she chose to meet Gillian and Ben as possible parents for her child.

When they met, the families exchanged stories about how their lives had led them to this point. Crystal's uncle described how a friend they saw at a restaurant had recently mentioned a "perfect couple" that might want to adopt his niece's child. But Crystal had already made the decision to meet another couple, her uncle told the friend.

Two days later that same friend called with an amazing story. Her niece and nephew were meeting with an expectant mom living with her aunt and uncle in San Diego. "That woman I ran into at the restaurant was your aunt," Crystal's uncle told Gillian and Ben.

Gillian cried; Crystal cried; even the adoption specialist cried. They spent the next six weeks getting to know each other. They also reached out to the expectant father of the baby to invite him to form a relationship with Ben and Gillian.

When Crystal went into labor, she sent a text to Gillian and told her she'd let them know when the baby was born and that she was ready for them to come to the hospital. After Crystal had some quiet time with her son, she invited Gillian and Ben to meet him. Once there, Gillian followed Crystal's lead and stayed close to Crystal to offer whatever help and support she needed.

The experience changed the way Ben and Gillian thought about adoption and especially open adoption. As they got to know Crystal and her extended family, they started to realize how much Crystal loved her baby and what love it took for her to decide to place him in their family. They have stayed in touch with her and the birth father through emails, phone calls, and pictures, even making a long trip to where Crystal had moved to visit her and the baby's birth father, assuring them they wanted to maintain a relationship.

When Gillian and Ben decided to try to adopt again, they approached it with a new perspective: They thought of the impact relinquishment would have on the baby's birth parents. They embraced the idea of a relationship with the birth parents of another child, and once they adopted again, they formed a relationship with their second child's birth family as well.

● ● ●

Emma and Robert had four children and dreamed of foster parenting, but they waited until their youngest son entered college. Enter LeAnne, who had experienced years of instability and turmoil. Her mother suffered from drug addiction, and her grandmother was at times physically and emotionally abusive. LeAnne's aunt, who had been unable to keep LeAnne with her, nonetheless had provided as much love and stability for her as she could. And then the family was uprooted by Hurricane Katrina.

LeAnne came into Emma and Robert's home through the foster system, but it wasn't long before they applied to adopt the energetic, passionate teenager. The adoption was finalized when LeAnne was fifteen.

LeAnne brought her own challenges, but after raising four teenagers, Emma and Robert took them in stride.

• • •

Makayla and Tyrone decided to pursue adoption and that they'd be open to parenting a child with special needs.

When they got a call about a couple six months pregnant and looking into adoption for their child, they were told testing suggested the baby would have Down syndrome and that ultrasounds showed a heart defect. Did Makayla and Tyrone want to be considered? They'd had enough experience with others with Down syndrome that they felt comfortable, and so they met with the expectant parents. They connected immediately, and the parents asked Makayla and Tyrone to parent their baby.

Christian's birth is forever etched in Makayla's mind. "When I first held him in my arms, I already had so much love for him, I just knew he was my son," she said. "That he had Down syndrome didn't matter."

Let's close this chapter on adoption with a first-person account from an adoptee who not only met her birth mother years after her adoption but benefited from the support of her adoptive parents.

While waiting to meet Londi, my birth mother, I felt anxious, nervous, and excited. I'd dreamed about this moment for a long time, and it was finally here.

Suddenly doubts crowded my mind. What if she wasn't who I thought she was? What if this went badly?

Over the years my adoptive family and I had come to know Londi and her family through letters and shared photos. We had a semi-open adoption and a growing relationship, but I had never met her in person.

When she walked into the room, I could tell she was nervous, too, which made me feel a little better. Maybe she had similar thoughts, anxieties, and doubts. But then we hugged, and all my worries disappeared.

Since then I have become close to Londi's family. Through the years I've attended her other children's birthday parties and sporting events and celebrated my birthday with them. My friendship with Londi is one of the most precious relationships in my life. Her family accepts me as their own, and, of course, I have my family, who love me unconditionally and want nothing but the best for me. They shared my excitement for building a lasting relationship with my birth mother. Every step of the way they have been at my side helping me cope with my questions and doubts.

───── Opening Your Heart ─────

- Do you know someone who was adopted or has adopted a child? How does their story factor into your overall understanding of adoption?

- What is your perception of adoption now after reading this chapter? Has it changed?

- What surprised you about open adoption or the issues best addressed before birth parents make an adoption plan or adoptive parents move forward with adoption? Why?

- What one or two stories in this chapter about adoption most captured your heart? How so?

- If you're thinking about adoption or supporting adoption, what type are you thinking about? Why does it interest you as opposed to other ways to answer the call?

———— PRAYING FOR MY CALL ————

Lord, I have so much to learn and consider about adoption—much more than I realized. Some of the ideas I had about adoption have altered. Give me the understanding, clarity, wisdom, and compassion I need to know how adoption fits into your call for me to care. If adoption is an area where you want me to serve, either by bringing a child into my home or by supporting adoptive or birth parents, guide me. Amen.

7

A Closer Look
at Domestic Adoption

A common misconception says most expectant mothers considering making a domestic adoption plan are teens with college plans, a steady boyfriend, and supportive parents. The reality is that women making adoption decisions are often in their twenties or early thirties, parenting other children, and alone, or at least not in an ongoing relationship. They may not have the emotional reserves to parent another child, or they may have a history of substance abuse or be involved in the child protection system, often coming to the attention of Child Protective Services because of abuse or neglect.

All these scenarios are examples of domestic adoption:

- A young woman learns she's pregnant after the baby's father is out of the picture.
- Parents feel they can't raise a child with serious medical or developmental challenges.
- A stepparent adopts a child whose parent has died or is absent because of divorce.

- Grandparents adopt grandchildren after they're removed from a birth mother's care because of abuse or neglect.
- Foster parents adopt a foster child whom they love and who is considered "hard to place" because of his or her age after the birth parents' parental rights are terminated.

Traditional Domestic Infant Adoption

Traditional domestic infant adoption, which is how most people think of adoption, involves a mom and sometimes a dad making an adoption plan and relinquishing a child at birth, with the baby coming into the care of the adoptive parents shortly thereafter. Sometimes, at the discretion of the birth parents, the adoptive parents are present at the birth of that child.

The number of infants available for adoption has dropped. Pregnancy rates are lower, possibly because of the accessibility of birth control but also possibly because of the availability of the morning-after pill. There is also a higher social acceptance of single parenting with many single moms choosing to parent, which may indeed be the best choice for that family.

Older Child Adoption

Older child adoption represents the greatest need in the United States. In 2017, more than 440,000 children were in the foster system in the United States, and nearly 20,000 aged out of the foster system without forever families. Over 100,000 of the children in foster care are available for adoption. And that's what brings us to adoption through the foster care system. [1]

The Adoption Journey through Foster Care

For some who want to adopt, the journey begins with foster care, which is by nature temporary. Some parents plan to only foster but

74

then move to adoption. Others plan to adopt through the foster care system, so they start the process with that goal in mind.

Let's be honest again, just as we were in the chapter about foster care: Foster parents, including those who want to adopt, can face an emotional journey. In most cases, children who come into foster care have been removed from homes where their safety was threatened by abuse or neglect. These kids are emotionally wounded and struggle with a variety of issues because of that wounding.

Be Aware of Potential Challenges

Not all foster-to-adopt placements end in adoption despite that being the goal for some foster parents. The child's parents may retain their rights after making changes necessary to keep their children safe. Reunification and family preservation is the first choice by law, policy, and practice if kids can be kept safe. Relatives may be able to raise the child and keep the child's family relationships intact. The child may have more needs than the foster parents can handle on a permanent basis.

Going into the process knowing the challenges they may face allows for better understanding as foster parents offer stability to vulnerable children.

The Process

Once parental rights are terminated or are on that path and foster parents express interest in adopting the children in their care, their adoption caseworker communicates with the child's social worker about next steps. Is the family the best fit for the child? Have they completed an adoption plan? Are resources available for the children and family—financial, educational, medical, counseling, and so on?

If a child or children are in a foster home where there are no plans to adopt, the social worker begins to look for potential adoptive parents, some of whom may already be foster parents.

Prospective adoptive parents hoping to adopt through the foster care system can also begin to search for a child or children via adoption exchanges. In Michigan, where Bethany Christian Services is headquartered, that resource is called MARE, the Michigan Adoption Resource Exchange. Other states have similar databases, and the countrywide database is AdoptUSKids.

MARE lists every child in the state who has been waiting for adoption for a significant amount of time. On average in Michigan, three hundred children are waiting at a time, with about three thousand kids becoming legally free to be adopted each year in Michigan alone. Foster parents can begin the process by asking about specific children they might foster with the intent to adopt.

Because birth parents are usually still involved and working toward reunification, occasionally they and foster parents meet in court situations or during supervised visitations as the birth parents work through the steps to retain the rights to their children. If reunification isn't successful, foster parents can begin the process to adopt the child or children. Birth parents, in turn, can be left feeling guilty that their actions precluded parenting and resentful toward those who care for and love their children. Or perhaps they just miss their kids.

A foster care licensing specialist describes how respectful and loving the relationship can be between foster/adoptive parents and birth parents. One of her goals is to help foster and birth families develop a positive relationship, and success usually depends on all parents' openness to being in relationship.

She witnessed an exchange between foster/adoptive parents and a birth father. He had been involved with Bethany before with his two other children, although reunification hadn't been successful. The children were adopted by their foster family, about whom the birth father spoke with respect and gratitude. The same family accepted placement of this father's youngest child when she came into foster care, so she could be with her siblings.

This can be a stressful situation as the birth parents grieve over termination of their rights; foster parents can be guarded as they anticipate birth parents being resentful about their role as parents of their children. In this case, the birth father was meeting the adoptive parents of his two older children, who were also foster parents of his youngest.

They met in the lobby after his visit with his daughter, greeting one another with smiles and hugs and talking for several minutes. The birth dad expressed gratitude to the foster mom for caring for his daughter and providing a forever family for his older children. She showed him pictures of the older kids and promised to make copies for him.

The parents probably had some anxiety about meeting each other for the first time after the adoption of the older two children, but they seemed to have made the decision to be respectful and mature, which in turn made the meeting natural and positive.

Challenges Abound, but . . .

Foster care adoptions can be challenging, intense, and emotional. Some children have been exposed to drugs, alcohol, or excessive stress before birth. The birth mom or dad may have mental health issues. There may be family history of illnesses, such as cystic fibrosis or Huntington's disease. Children may have Down syndrome or other genetic syndromes, autism spectrum disorders, sensory integration issues, cerebral palsy, or epilepsy.

Despite their diagnostic labels, however, most are regular kids dealt a tough hand who need stability, acceptance, and love. We love to hear about families who have welcomed children into their homes as foster children and then welcomed them into their hearts as their children, without the distinction of adoption versus biology. We love to hear about families demonstrating God's grace to one another. After all, it's all about the best care possible for vulnerable children.

Let's look at three of those stories now.

Chelsey always knew she would adopt a child with special needs. As a single parent of three children, she provided weekend respite for families who had children with disabilities. When the time came, she began her journey by attending foster care classes. Her goal was crystal clear: "I want to take in the kids nobody else thinks they can handle because of medical problems."

Eventually she was asked a big question. Would she be willing to jump right into adoption rather than fostering? Her answer was yes.

Chelsey is now mom to Priya, who suffers a wide range of disabilities caused by shaken baby syndrome. Chelsey and her children love this little girl, and it's clear she loves them too.

• • •

While browsing the internet, Gina happened upon an adoption site with pictures of little boys needing families. Soon she and her husband, Dylan, actively pursued adoption, focusing on older children.

Noah, age ten, became part of their forever family. Six months later, Gina and Dylan learned Noah's younger brother, Liam, would need a home as well. He was four years younger than Noah and had significant medical needs. After Liam's foster mother's adoption plans fell through, Gina and Dylan invited him to their home for a weekend with his brother.

"I have two brothers and can't imagine not growing up with them. How would Noah feel not growing up with his brother?" Dylan said. They made the call to adopt Liam.

Gina notes how adopting older children has its own specialness. "Everyone wants cute babies," she said, "but older children are so special."

• • •

Connie has cared for medically fragile foster children for twenty-three years, first as a single woman and then with her husband, Bill. They came to know James after he was removed from his family because of abuse and neglect. He was living in a group home when he was diagnosed with bone cancer.

Bill and Connie welcomed him into their home as a foster child. By this time, he'd been in institutional care for four years and was recovering from cancer treatments. He was totally withdrawn, curled up in a

The Importance of Permanence

The Honorable Kathleen A. Feeney, assigned to the Family Division of the Seventeenth Circuit Court in Grand Rapids, Michigan, has seen family situations that break her heart and situations that cause her and her staff to weep with joy.

"We always ask ourselves what is the best thing for the child with respect to permanence," said Judge Feeney, who was appointed to the bench in 2000. "At every stage of the game we try to determine, based on all the factors available, whether this child needs permanence involving reunification or not involving reunification. How do you balance a child's desire to go back to family with the trauma that has gone on there?"

No hard and fast rules exist for how we measure permanence, she said, but we often look to sources such as the Child Custody Act and its twelve factors that define the "best interests of the child." Factors include love and emotional ties between the parties involved; capacity of parties involved to give the child love and guidance and provide the child with food, clothing, and medical care; mental and physical health of parties involved; reasonable preferences of the child; and domestic violence.

"Kids have to have permanence at critical points in their lives," Feeney said. "The younger the child, the faster you have to work to achieve that permanence. Parents say they'll get better or mom says she'll stop seeing that guy. But there comes a point in time when kids need permanency."

Federal and Michigan law require a permanency planning review hearing within 365 days of removal from the home. At that review hearing, decisions are made about whether to move toward termination, give parents more time for treatment or training, or keep the child in foster care.

"We have to talk about the permanency goal for this child," Feeney said. "We do everything we can to make sure they're safe when they go back home after foster care. We're not looking for perfect parents; we're looking for adequate parents who want what's best for their child. We celebrate when the cycle stops."

ball. He soon responded to the love from his foster parents, and within months he became a funny, delightful, charming young man. His foster parents decided to pursue adoption.

Then his cancer returned, and it was terminal. They finalized the adoption anyway—because families are not just for those who are well.

"I got to take care of James," Connie said. "I know he felt completely loved when he died. He was surrounded by people who loved him."

Domestic adoption through the foster system—fostering to adopt—is growing as more people recognize that caring for vulnerable children means adopting children who are older, who are considered hard to place, or who have siblings who should be adopted with them.

Children in foster care are often those who need families most. Intercountry adoption may be your call, and we'll cover that type of adoption next. But before you move forward with an intercountry adoption, also pray about the vulnerable children close to home to ensure you go where God leads.

After years of infertility, Quinn and Marcy were contemplating intercountry adoption. They reconsidered after learning domestic adoption would allow them to adopt a child in their own city.

When they got a call about a two-year-old boy whose mother was considering placing him for adoption, they were advised to go ahead with a trip they had planned to Washington, D.C. Upon arriving, they got a voicemail saying the mother had brought Eli in that morning and wanted him placed that day.

Thanks to a system of interim care, Eli had a place to stay until they got back. Then came another call. The birth mother also wanted to place Eli's six-month-old brother, Owen. Would they consider adopting a second child?

Two weeks later the two boys arrived at their new home with their excited adoptive parents. "We can't imagine not having two. They're great together," Marcy said.

Every Child Deserves a Home

The Multiethnic Placement Act (MEPA) of 1994 as amended prohibits the delay or denial of any adoption or foster care placement due to race, color, or national origin of the child or foster/adoptive parents.

Bethany Christian Services is dedicated to compliance with MEPA, which is why we don't have potential adoptive or foster parents specify racial makeup of a child they are open to fostering or adopting.

All children of all races, colors, and national origins deserve a forever home with a family to love them.

OPENING YOUR HEART

- If you're thinking about domestic adoption, are you open to children who are harder to place, such as an older child or child with special needs? Perhaps a sibling group? Why or why not?
- Were you shocked by how many children in foster care age out of the system without a home and family of their own? Does this instill in you a sense of urgency on their behalf? How so?
- Do you know anyone who aged out of the foster care system without a forever family? How did that affect them? Or how do you imagine aging out of the system without a family would have affected you?
- If you hear the call to adopt, would you consider foster care as a road to adoption? Why or why not?
- How might your church support domestic adoption of all kinds?

―――― PRAYING FOR MY CALL ――――

Lord, help me keep my heart open to the needs of all vulnerable children around the world. They all deserve a home. Yet so many are right in my backyard. Show me if this is the area you want me to explore. Don't let me close my eyes to the need. Show me how I can help one, two, or many in service to you and to them. Amen.

8

A Closer Look
at Intercountry Adoption

Intercountry adoption is the process of adopting children from another country. The goal of intercountry adoption is to provide a permanent family for a child when all other options for permanency have been exhausted.

Like all types of adoption, intercountry adoption is about families for children, not children for families. And it is only one of the options to be considered when looking at permanence for children. The number of children joining families in the US through adoption from other countries has dropped considerably for a variety of reasons, including the strengthening of child protection systems in the children's home countries. While in the past there were many infants eligible for adoption, now the children for whom intercountry adoption is the best option are usually older and often bring with them various needs and challenges. Thousands of children are still waiting for permanent families.

In 2016, the US State Department issued visas for 5,372 children to be adopted into forever families in the United States. Over 40 percent came from China, with the next largest numbers coming from the Democratic Republic of Congo (less than 7 percent) and Ukraine and South Korea (both at around 5 percent).[1]

Special Needs

Every child is special, and every child, whether biological or adopted, will require parenting to whatever needs they have. That is certainly true for children eligible for intercountry adoption, and their needs may not be fully known at the time of adoption. We know that these children have experienced loss and have too often lived in institutions rather than in family-based care. We also know that many may have physical conditions or health concerns, histories of trauma, and other adverse childhood experiences. They are often older and have siblings to be adopted with them, but like all children, they need the love and support of a family to call their own.

Consider the following accounts:

Darius and Erica thought adoption was a natural fit for their family after having two biological children. First came Daniel from Guatemala, and then came May from China. They were apprehensive about adopting May because she had a serious heart condition that would require extensive surgery to correct. But they prayed and left the outcome to God. May joined their family, and after a complicated heart surgery, she made a full recovery.

Still, their third intercountry adoption brought familiar jitters as they boarded a plane bound for China to unite with their new daughter, whom they would name Violet. She had been diagnosed with cerebral palsy and had spent most of her young life in a physical rehabilitation hospital.

While her physical challenges meant a challenging road ahead, and she's taken a step back now and then, Violet has made huge steps forward. Her bright and joyful outlook is an inspiration to everyone.

• • •

Megan and Parker began their intercountry adoption journey thinking they'd wait about a year, but they waited four years for their daughter, Jennifer. As hard as that time was, they believe the wait was worth the outcome. Their original plan was to adopt an infant, but as time passed they realized the children waiting for adoption were either older or had medical challenges. They felt God leading them to an older child with identified needs who needed a family ready and able to meet those needs with them. In changing their idea about adoption, they had to reevaluate why they really wanted to adopt a child and what their expectations of her or him would be.

"The day we submitted our paper work, we received photos of our daughter," Megan said. The three-year-old little girl had a cleft lip and palate. She had undergone two surgeries in China and would need many more. Nevertheless, her new parents and older brother were thrilled to have her become part of their family.

Motivations and Expectations for Overseas Adoption

Welcoming a child home through intercountry adoption can be a beautiful and enriching experience, although an experience prospective adoptive parents must reflect on carefully as they consider growing their family through this type of adoption. Just as with any answer to the call to care, they need to think through their motivations and expectations.

When one considers this type of adoption, motivations can range from truly helping a child to being inspired by others who have adopted children internationally. Do the parents want to embrace the diversity of God's creation and be a family for a child who needs one? Or is their motivation one of those cautioned about in previous chapters, such as to fill a void left by infertility or the loss of a child, or to alleviate guilt when others have prodded them to reach out in this way?

Considering expectations is the next step. The late Dr. Karyn Purvis, from Texas Christian University's Institute of Child Development, whom we've mentioned before, described the challenge of parents to create safety, security, and a nurturing environment for vulnerable children.[2] Do prospective parents expect a child to fit seamlessly into their family with no regret or sense of loss about leaving family and homeland? Do they expect family members to accept a child from another country?

Do they have any idea what these children may have experienced?

Here are some scenarios children eligible for adoption from another country might have gone through, drawn from real cases:

- An older girl becomes available for adoption after she's rescued from a labor trafficking situation. She'd been promised an education if she moved to the city, but instead she was forced to work in a clothing factory for fifteen hours a day.
- A little girl has spent the first year of her life in a crib in an orphanage, with little physical touch from adults and even less interaction with other children.
- An older boy is rescued from the streets, where he had to fight for every bite of food—and occasionally for his life.
- Twin girls are abandoned by their mother on the steps of a church. Not only could she not care for them, but they are in a society that values boys, not girls.

As you can imagine, childhood events such as these make an impact on children for their entire lives. Understanding the impact can be frightening, because we don't know exactly what the impact will be on a child's development and, consequently, how they react to the world. Adjusting expectations accordingly and receiving training to deal with grief, anger, meltdowns, attachment challenges, fear, and food hoarding can help everyone in the family.

Unique Considerations and Cautions

Intercountry adoption brings with it unique dimensions, cautions, and opportunities. Here are a few of them, directed to anyone thinking about this type of adoption:

- The country from which you adopt sets the rules for intercountry adoption. United States agencies have no control over their rules, paper work requirements, fees, or care standards.

- Intercountry adoption usually requires at least one trip to the child's home country, sometimes two, depending on the country. Your child will return with you on the last trip. These visits can last days, weeks, or months. Consider carefully whether you can afford to travel and to take the time off work. Also, if you have other children, think about who will care for them while you're away.

- Don't speak negatively about the medical care your child has received in their country of origin. You may feel it's not up to the standards you want, but that's likely more an issue of resources than of caring. Countries have different resources, cultural practices, and behavioral health practices.

- Don't speak ill about the lack of care your child received. Overworked orphanage workers or foster parents care about the children and are thrilled each time one finds a forever home. One family adopted a child from South Korea whose foster mother had cared for her for almost a year. The foster mom loved that little girl well, which was apparent when they met. Her new parents were so grateful, and like other foster parents, her foster grieved her loss even as she celebrated that the little one had been adopted by a family who would love her and get her the medical care she needed.

- If you know you want to adopt multiple children, sibling groups may be an appropriate choice. It's important for siblings to stay together whenever possible.

The Process

Intercountry adoptions require much of the same process as domestic adoptions: home studies, paper work, education, medical exams, criminal record checks, financial stability and mental health evaluations, and awareness about the experiences these children could be bringing with them, in this case from their homelands. Add to that meeting the requirements of their country and completing a dossier and all the documentation and fingerprinting required for United States Citizenship and Immigration Services approval.

Intercountry adoption is a wonderful way to care for the world's orphaned and vulnerable children who lack the protection of a family. So many children around the world—orphaned or abandoned—deserve love and a forever family.

Here are four more stories about intercountry adoption you may find inspiring.

Little Gabra was born in Ethiopia into extreme poverty. His mother couldn't care for him, so at six years old he was moved to an orphanage. The caretakers tried their best, but institutional care is not good for children. Gabra learned to stand up for himself to get what he wanted, yet he hoped and yearned for a family.

Jon and Reese saw Gabra's profile in early 2014 and began praying, along with their twelve children, that Gabra could join their family. A year and a half later, Jon and Reese flew to Ethiopia to bring him home.

Gabra was always on alert and couldn't sleep without several lights on. "At the beginning," Reese said, "he felt he needed to look out for himself and defend himself. We reminded him that we are a family, and that this is a safe environment, but we also knew he needed to experience our family as safe. That took time."

Reese and Jon were well equipped with training and support from their agency to help guide Gabra through the transition of joining their family. Today he has overcome some of his fears and has a new sense of calm. He just needs a night-light now, because he knows he is with family and he can trust his mom and dad and the security of their home. His anxiety was not because of his new parents or what they provided but because of his history and his self-protective response. Changing that takes time.

* * *

Christa had dreamed about intercountry adoption for years, but then a three-week mission trip to Uganda solidified that dream. After returning home, she talked and prayed about it with her husband, Dan. They decided to pursue adoption from Ethiopia when they learned Ugandan adoptions were on hold while the Ugandan government reviewed its adoption process.

About eight months after Christa and Dan started the process, Debre, nine, and Berihun, eleven, were home with them and welcomed by three older brothers. The family had been praying that the other children who had been in the group home with Debre and Berihun would find families too. A few years later, they learned only one teen was left from that group, and they felt God calling them to adopt him. Debre and Berihun were excited about the possibility of Kaleb joining their family, because they thought of him as their brother already.

Christa and Dan were excited to bring Kaleb home. Now the family hears a lot of happy Amharic spoken!

* * *

Adele and Jared adopted their son from Ethiopia, and several years later they decided they would try to adopt from there again. They filled out the paper work to apply to adopt and begin the home study process. Then they sent it off and sat back, praying, waiting, and looking through pictures of waiting children.

Adele came across the picture of a little girl from South Africa, but they'd already paid the necessary fees to Ethiopia. Jared told her he'd been asking God to show them the face of their next child and had clearly heard God say it would be within a month.

When a referral didn't come from Ethiopia, he asked when Adele had first seen the picture of the girl. It was within that month time frame! They set the money issue aside and had paper work presented to South Africa. Their faith and a grant helped bring their new daughter into their home.

* * *

Sam and Kari, who would be considered older parents, were told they met the requirements to adopt a child from China. Now they could begin their home study and the process of completing a dossier once their home study was approved.

When they received a list of waiting children, they looked into the eyes of one toddler and knew they would seek to adopt her. Four months later they were in China to bring home this little girl who had a cleft palate that would need repair once she was in the United States.

Adopting a toddler after raising three sons and entering their fifties was a radical move. But two years later, they welcomed a thirteen-year-old from Ethiopia into their family. Adopting a child out of birth order brought different challenges for them and especially for their daughter, but it was worthwhile. Sam and Kari are thrilled to say age is not a limiting factor when it comes to caring for vulnerable children.

Opening Your Heart

- If you're considering intercountry adoption, what are your motivations? Your expectations?

- List any fears or concerns you have, and then talk to someone who has adopted from another country or to an intercountry adoption specialist.

- Are you open to adopting a child with special needs since many children available for adoption from another country have special needs?

- Are you ready for the unknown? For an unexpected diagnosis, behavior, or challenge? If not, how do you think you can best prepare for that possibility besides receiving training?

- How open are you to learning about the culture of your child's country of origin? Are you willing to educate your child about their country of origin?

- How might your church support intercountry adoption?

───── PRAYING FOR MY CALL ─────

God, the world is full of vulnerable children who need some-one to give them a loving home, and many of them have special needs. If you're calling me to be a part of giving a home to or finding homes for children who live somewhere else in the world, show me. Whatever you want me to do on behalf of children around the world, give me the guidance I need. Amen.

9

Acknowledging Loss and Grief

Adoption is born of loss. It is a positive and life-affirming choice, but that doesn't negate the fact that there is loss for everyone in the adoption triad: the birth parents, the adoptive parents, and the adopted child.

Birth parents grieve that they won't be parenting their children and be with them daily. The adoptive couple grieves the loss of the physical experience of pregnancy and birth for their adopted child and perhaps missing their early years, and infertility has its own losses to be acknowledged and grieved. Adoptees lose genetic connection with family and all that entails. And these are only some of the things members of the adoption triad might grieve.

Here's one mother's story about not only her adoption plan experience, but her grief:

When twenty-seven-year-old Amber learned she was pregnant, her first thought was to have an abortion. Her three kids already kept her busy; she got very little help from their father. And no one would ever know she'd become pregnant again. But she wasn't sure she could go through with an abortion.

When a friend shared that one of her children was adopted, Amber began to consider adoption, but she also wanted to explore all her options other than abortion. She met regularly with a pregnancy counselor to explore what each option might mean to her, such as what support she would need if she parented this child herself. Soon she realized adoption was the right choice for her and her unborn baby, and she courageously began the difficult journey of placing her child with another mom and dad.

When Amber started looking through adoptive parent profiles, she immediately focused on Sean and Allison. She met with the couple several times and even spent a night in their home to get to know them better and gain a sense of what her child's life might be like.

Since baby Christopher was born, Amber has visited with him and his adoptive parents every other month, and they email regularly. Allison shares pictures and videos often. At Amber's most recent visit, her other kids joined her. "I have cried buckets of tears, and I think about him every day," Amber said. "But I know he's with a family who was ready to care for him."

Because of her experience and how affirming her relationship has been with Sean and Allison, Amber has become a vocal advocate for adoption. She's shared her story in the local newspaper during National Adoption Month in November.

"It helps me to know I can communicate with his parents and that I'll know about my son and he'll know about me. But nothing can fill the hole that tore my heart when I handed him over," Amber said. "All I ever wanted to be was a mom, but I had to think of him and my other kids instead of just me this time. It was not my time to be his mom; it was Allison's."

Amber acknowledged the loss she felt, understanding that it was okay to grieve even though she chose adoption and communicated with her child's new parents. Acknowledging and grieving the losses of relinquishment and adoption is important, however those losses are perceived. We can understand the risk of what Dr. Kenneth Doka, an expert in grief counseling and therapy, has termed "disenfranchised grief"—when the right to give voice to loss and be supported in that grief by one's social support system is denied.[1] Disenfranchised grief is a risk for everyone involved in an adoption.

How Open Adoption Can Help

The field of adoption has been slow to change. However, adoption is a dynamic system, and adoptive parents need to use agencies that serve equally the adoption triad.

Open adoption doesn't reduce grief. But knowing about their child and his or her new family can be comforting to birth parents even amid feelings of loss and grief. Dr. Pauline Boss, a leading therapist in the area of family stress, first identified ambiguous loss as a loss where there is a lack of knowledge or information about loved ones, something very much at risk without contact between parent and child.[2] Grief discounted or denied risks expression in other ways, such as depression, anger, physical illness, or self-medication through substance use.

The more open and honest adoption climate is an improvement. As mentioned earlier, closed adoptions—when birth parents relinquish all rights, don't know the adoptive parents, and don't communicate with them—have become rare. And the possibility of maintaining such secrecy or lack of contact on a long-term basis has become less and less likely, given the growth of social media and multiple ways of connecting with people via the internet. Some domestic adoptions have been referred to as semi-open (limited communication between birth and adoptive parents) or mediated (communication goes through the adoption agency).

While some families believe mediated contact is preferable, fully disclosed adoptions—when relationships with healthy boundaries are formed—often best meet the needs of everyone. Like any other relationship, adoption relationships are not always easy; they can have challenges. Honest communication and support from adoption professionals when needed can help everyone involved navigate challenges today rather than delaying them for the future.

Managing Grief

Acknowledgment of loss and grief and support for the relationships in adoption can help everyone involved establish the healthiest relationships possible for the benefit of all, but especially for the person at the center, the one everyone loves: the child.

Let's turn to a story about an adoptive mother who recognized not only a birth mother's grief but her own.

Savannah and Ty anticipated welcoming a child into their family through adoption. After the birth of their daughter six years earlier, conceiving again had eluded them, although the cause was unknown. They had been so excited to meet Becky, an expectant twentysomething mother, and her family as she wrestled with the decision about whether to make an adoption plan.

When Becky's baby was born, Savannah and Ty went to the hospital to support Becky and meet the baby. Savannah was suddenly overcome with grief. Talking with her social worker through tears, she said she felt grief for Becky. But then she realized she was also grieving for herself because she couldn't experience pregnancy and birth again.

Support throughout the grief process is an important part of the adoption journey, and counseling staff understand the need to listen to those experiencing loss and to be a companion in their grief. No matter the circumstances, relinquishing a child isn't easy.

Willow was in the process of divorcing her husband of fifteen years when she became pregnant as the result of a brief relationship with another man. She didn't know how she could care for a baby and her three other children as a single mother.

She scheduled an abortion despite misgivings, and then the night before she canceled. But now what? The conversations with her now ex-husband and her children were as difficult as she imagined, and she had no idea what to do.

A friend told her she'd placed a child for adoption years before. Willow reached out to an adoption agency and learned about the process, receiving significant support from her pregnancy counselor, Joanna.

"Joanna and I became close," Willow said. "I could be myself with her. I could tell her I felt conflicted, scared, and uncertain. Everywhere else I had to be strong for people, like my kids. I wouldn't have made it through that time without this help. She also helped me find additional support for my children, who would, in many ways, be losing a sibling."

She was initially uncertain about an open adoption, thinking it might be too painful to have contact with the baby. But she grew excited as she sorted through profiles of potential families, eventually settling on Brian and Joy.

Giving birth was bittersweet. She had spent time alone before she went into labor to feel the finality of the situation, taking in the reality that she would be saying good-bye and grieving. But through Joanna, Willow had connected with a local church that became a real support for her. Elizabeth, a member of that church and part of Willow's support group, became her labor coach. Joanna, Brian, and Joy were there for the birth as well.

Willow is at peace, certain she made the right choice for her son, and grateful that though they will always live with the loss, she and her children have a support system to help them.

Children Grieve Too

Those who experience relinquishment and adoption have losses that must be grieved as well. Counseling may be the best course of action. Even the youngest of children needs help to work through their feelings of loss, especially when they don't know how to talk through that grief. While grief is normal and we can often work through it without counseling, everyone needs a safe and supportive environment where they can share and process their emotions.

This next story is about a young teenager who received help in managing his grief, not only from his own grandmother but from counseling and his adoptive parents as well.

Thirteen-year-old Damien was close to his grandmother, whom he called his mom. After all, she was the one who loved him and raised him. When she became terminally ill, Damien became her caregiver. But when she could no longer keep him in her home, he had no choice but to enter the foster care system.

Enter Carter and Brittany, who had decided to get foster care training and let God decide whether they would adopt through foster care. They expected someone younger when they received the call about Damien, who by this time was fourteen and needed a new foster home. But they were sure they were to be his foster parents when they heard his story.

Before long, Carter and Brittany had grown to love Damien and wanted him to stay permanently. Adoption, however, wasn't what Damien and his grandmother wanted right then, made clear as they accepted some counseling to deal with the many decisions they needed to make. Damien wanted to be loyal to his grandmother, but just before she died and after getting to know Carter and Brittany, she asked Damien to let them adopt him.

Everyone struggled with the loss, and both Damien and his grandmother worked through the grief, but now Damien is in a forever home with a family to support him through the rest of his teenage years. And Carter and Brittany feel blessed because they were able to get to know Damien's grandmother, to see her love for him, and to experience her courage. They can share in Damien's memories of her because they have their own, joining him in honoring her memory and all that she was to him.

──── Opening Your Heart ────

- What personal grief experiences would you bring to the adoption triad?
- What surprised you about the loss and grief that are experienced in the adoption triad?
- Whom in the adoption triad do you identify with the most? Why?
- Do you feel, or have you ever felt, any sense of judgment toward adults who elect to make an adoption plan rather than raise their child after an unintended pregnancy? Why or why not?
- How might you react differently toward birth parents, adoptive parents, or an adopted child after reading this chapter?

──── Praying for My Call ────

Lord, I will never know what someone else is experiencing until I take the time to understand what they face. As I consider how to answer your call to care, give me empathy and an open heart toward all those involved in the quest to love and care for a child through adoption. Never let me be blind to parents and children who are experiencing loss and grief. Amen.

PART THREE

EMBRACING FAMILY PRESERVATION

10

Tapping into Family Preservation Programs

As explained earlier, the first goal of those within the family care community is to keep a child within the family of origin or within a kinship relationship. Keeping a child in a family with genetic connections and history reduces his or her experience of loss and disruption, which can have long-term implications.

Some families, however, need help when their strength or resources are low and their support system, if they have one, is unable to help. They can voluntarily take advantage of informal help or have court-ordered and trained staff to work with them to keep the family together if they become involved in the public child welfare system.

In a later chapter we'll talk more about community programs that assist families and children who need help, but here are a few specific examples of programs that help make it possible for families to stay together.

HOMEBUILDERS is an intervention program designed to strengthen families to prevent avoidable out-of-home placement and to return children from care to their families.

Family Group Decision-Making is both a home-based program and an approach that empowers families within their extended family structures to work cooperatively with each other and the community to resolve issues that have resulted from abuse/neglect investigations.

Churches can provide many services in a less formal way to families who seek help. They can also offer friendship, spiritual growth, and worship opportunities. More information on how churches can help families is in chapter 16.

Safe Families for Children (SFFC), highlighted in previous chapters, is a national movement founded in 2003 that gives hope to families in crisis and out of options. The program is not an option when children are unsafe because of abuse or neglect; it essentially expands a family's support system in time of crisis or high need.

To avoid their children entering foster care, families use this program for temporary care of their children while the adult or adults find a home, a job, or emotional stability or while they access needed medical care.

Bethany Christian Services provides support in partnership with more than forty churches for SFFC in multiple states. SFFC is truly a movement of the church that partners with professional social workers and counseling staff to ensure that families are prepared to meet the needs of children and the potential challenges that come with family hosting. Families contact us when they need help, and we connect them with trained host families to welcome the children. Parents are free to visit their kids, and often host families build relationships with the parents and maintain them even after the crisis no longer exists.

Here's the story of how one couple and their church answered the call to care through SFFC and another story about how one young mother was helped by the SFFC program.

With three young children at home, Hanh and Chinh couldn't go on overseas mission trips or volunteer for many of the service projects at church. Then they heard about Safe Families for Children and knew they had found their niche.

Since becoming a volunteer host family, Hanh and Chinh have welcomed eleven children into their home. Their second hosting was a six-year-old boy who stayed a week when his mother fled a domestic violence situation and needed someone to care for her son while she resettled. Hanh and the mom talked every day and forged a relationship they still have today.

"So many of these parents are desperate," Hanh said. "It's hard to imagine having no one to turn to for help in the midst of a crisis."

● ● ●

Shortly after moving to a new state, Liz suffered a severe health breakdown. Unable to work full-time, she fell behind on her rent, and after a ten-day hospitalization, during which her two-year-old son stayed with her parents in her former state, she found herself homeless. She was twenty-six years old and still far from well. She was also five months pregnant by her son's father, who left after she refused to abort her second child. She was all alone. And she was terrified. What would become of her, her son, and her unborn child?

With her son still with his grandparents, Liz slept that night at a mission and was told to leave at five the next morning. She returned to work and for days slept in her office after everyone had left.

Afraid to tell her parents of her circumstances, once she got paid, Liz retrieved her son and the two lived at a homeless shelter for several months. There she learned of a free daycare center, which provided the help she needed to land full-time employment. In due course, she and her son moved into a new residence.

Knowing that Liz would still lack a means of caring for her son once the baby was born, a caseworker at the daycare center gave Liz a brochure about Safe Families for Children. "I tossed the brochure to the side, reluctant to let a stranger care for my baby," Liz said. But when her daughter was born, further health issues forced her to call for help.

"The workers at the agency that sponsored SFFC were wonderful. They were kind, caring, and patient. They took the time to explain the extensive background checks they had to perform on a candidate for SFFC. They gave me thorough information about the host mother they had for my son. It was like I already knew her before I walked in the room to meet her face-to-face."

The next day, Liz met with her SFFC family coach and Sonya, the woman who would care for her son for the next thirty days. "They made me feel comfortable. We had an hour to talk everything over and get paper work signed, and I was able to watch Sonya interact with my son. Sonya had a crib and toys and everything together before he arrived. We communicated daily about his adjustment, and I frequently spoke with him to tell him good-night."

A month later, with her health improved and her daughter a little older, Liz resumed care for her son. A raise at work came a while later, and today Liz and her children are doing well.

Look in Your State, City, or Town

As we'll explore in chapter 17, states and local communities have safety nets for children and families, as do most smaller towns. Search out the services in your area that assist the families and children who need help, and see what holes you might be able to help fill. Everyone needs somewhere to find help.

—————— OPENING YOUR HEART ——————

- Has your family or a family you know ever needed help to stay together or thrive? What difference did that help make?

- What programs or services that provide a safety net for vulnerable families and children do you know about in your community?

- Does your church help children and families who need help? If not, what do you think holds it back? What do you think could move it forward?
- Does one of the programs mentioned in this chapter or a program like it appeal to you? How so?
- How might God already be calling you to help preserve a family or families?

––––––– PRAYING FOR MY CALL –––––––

God, I can't assume every family I see will remain intact without help. Make it clear if you're calling me to play even one small part to help keep families together, perhaps through a program that already exists. I commit to learning what programs are available in my community so if I encounter a family that needs help, I'll know where to suggest they turn. Amen.

11

Creating Support Groups

It would be easier for agencies to see couples through an adoption and then leave them to it once the child is legally theirs. It would be much less demanding to ignore the family needs and dynamics that put kids in foster care in the first place or families with children who have special needs, right?

But that's not what God calls believers to do. He calls us to wade into the mess and see how we can help. Part of that mandate is offering and helping others offer support for the journey, and one way we can do that is with support groups.

Support groups come in all shapes and sizes and cover all possible topics, with many degrees of structure and leadership. At its most basic, a support group is a gathering of people with common experiences who are seeking help and fellowship to assist them in managing their situations well.

Types of Support Groups

We have all probably experienced some form of formal or informal support group. For young moms it could be a group that meets weekly at a park or at a home for playdates for the kids and friendship for the moms. More formal groups such as MOPS (Mothers of Preschoolers) exist as well.

Adoptive moms or dads can meet informally for lunch or dinner once a month or attend weekly sessions set up by agencies. Parents can gather for educational information via organizations, or they can attend a Sunday school class specifically for younger or older parents.

Birth parents can also meet with support groups, whether informally or formally, to find others who have faced similar experiences, loss, and healing.

Foster parents, adoptive parents, birth parents, parents whose children are in out-of-home care or who may be soon, and parents of children with special needs, as well as grandparents, siblings, and children themselves can all be encouraged to find a community of people to help them along the journey.

The Advantages

The advantages of support groups for children and parents are many. Children learn social skills, such as sharing and taking turns, as they engage with other kids. Intercountry adoptees and those whose races differ from their parents' can be encouraged when they see other kids just like them with parents just like theirs.

Foster and adoptive parents can get advice on everything from handling awkward questions from strangers to dealing with dysregulated emotions in public places (when the child has a meltdown in a store, at church, in a family setting, etc.). They can get health care advice and information for specific needs; discuss their feelings, even anger or depression; and share their joys and victories. Support group members can advocate for others in the group via their connections as well as reach out to those connections for understanding of behaviors, the adoption processes, and even regulations.

Stories like these illustrate how support groups can make a difference:

Maria attended a support group for adoptive mothers after she and her husband adopted two brothers from Ukraine. The boys, ages two and four, had spent most of their lives in an orphanage. The older boy was having trouble attaching to his new parents. Maria came to her support group distraught, wondering if she'd ever connect with her son.

Another mom in the group had experienced the same thing with her adopted daughter. She recommended several strategies Maria could try, and she also suggested counseling for the family. Maria left the group that day with hope.

● ● ●

Luke and Karen's daughter became pregnant at twenty while still in college. When she told her parents that she was making an adoption plan, they weren't sure what to say. This was their first grandchild, but it was their daughter's decision. Should they offer to raise the child? Should they stay quiet? They wondered how to process the information and back her decision.

They knew several people at a Christian adoption agency, and they talked to them about how their daughter might make an adoption plan. When the friends sensed their ambivalence, they recommended a support group for birth grandparents whose children make adoption plans.

Luke and Karen found the help they needed to embrace and understand their daughter's plans and to process their own feelings of loss without trying to make them their daughter's responsibility.

● ● ●

Bethany Christian Services started a support group for adoptive dads, inviting half a dozen dads to participate. The group talked about the needs of adopted children, the needs of their wives, trauma histories, older children already in the home, and discipline issues. After meeting for six months, the group had grown to a dozen men. Two of the dads began taking leadership roles and soon oversaw the group, and a second group was formed, inviting more dads to participate.

● ● ●

Corine and Josh were immersed in foster parenting, taking in sibling groups for two to three weeks at a time. Because they hadn't parented before, they joined a foster parent support group that met once a week. The group had members with children of their own, older members, and experienced foster parents.

When Josh and Corine faced intense sibling rivalry during a placement, they brought the dilemma to their support group. The advice they received helped them through the difficult placement, and they were able to help the siblings better navigate their differences.

● ● ●

Carlos had lost his wife to illness, leaving him to raise his three preteen daughters alone. Having only brothers, he was clueless about how to handle the ups and downs of a girl's life. He began to attend a support group for single fathers offered through his large church. The first several meetings were uncomfortable because Carlos tends to be shy, but he began to get to know the other men and open up.

The men laughed together over the antics of their children, cried as they mourned their spouses, and prayed for God's help and presence during the child-rearing years. When Carlos's oldest daughter turned thirteen, the men and their kids joined them for a bonfire and birthday cake. His daughters seemed to come out of their shells as they played with the younger children and laughed at the goofy games.

After a year or so in the group, Carlos began to take a leadership role. Eventually he became the leader and was able to help other men on their journeys.

● ● ●

Darlene and Wyatt adopted Peter, whose parents had released him for adoption when they found he had Down syndrome, a diagnosis they felt unable to handle. They took classes on what to expect when adopting as well as classes on how to care for and parent a child with special needs. Their agency also linked them to resources in their community.

In addition, they participated in a support group for parents of children with special needs for three years, eventually deciding to adopt a second child with special needs. They learned how to handle medical issues specific to Down syndrome, how to advocate for the best educational opportunities, and how to navigate the many questions from curious people.

· · ·

Theresa and her husband were planning to adopt via the foster care system, and toward that end they were licensed to provide foster care. Their first placement, two brothers and a sister, started out rough. The children acted out, angry at having been taken from their mom, used to taking care of themselves, and worried about their mom, who had been addicted to drugs their entire lives.

Theresa was at a loss. She had taken classes and read up on the issues involved in foster care, but this was her first placement. Was she providing the kids the space they needed? The love and discipline they needed? She felt overwhelmed by the emotional and physical needs of the children.

Fortunately, Theresa was part of a foster care support group that met every other week. She broke down in tears at one gathering while sharing her fears and frustrations. The women gathered around her for hugs and shared tears and prayer. They offered advice and suggestions, but mostly they listened and loved her.

She left the gathering calmer, stronger, and ready to face what lay ahead. The next weeks were still tough, but things slowly improved. The children stayed with the family for fourteen months, during which time their mother was admitted to a drug treatment inpatient program. In the end, the family was reunified.

Who Can Start a Support Group?

Agencies can bring together these groups in a formal setting. Often invitations are extended and accepted, with staff leading the group and directing conversations and choosing topics to discuss. Hopefully the group coalesces and grows organically, with group members eventually moving into leadership roles. These groups usually meet at agency offices or in area churches.

Churches can also offer support groups with specific meeting times at the church and leadership from within the church. The gatherings can be more formal—topic schedules, guest speakers, meeting formats, childcare—or less formal. Structure, however, is generally good within church support groups.

Best Practices

If you or your church is interested in starting a support group, here are three best practices:

1. Invite people you think are interested to an informal discussion about what they would like to see in a support group. Ask how you can help them.
2. Listen to their needs and wants. This is a support group for *them*; what you think such a group should be may not be what they need.
3. Make the group participant directed, not leader directed. Let the group decide where to go and how to get there.

Families do better with support from professionals and others who have similar experiences and a heart to help. A heart to help also requires wisdom to discern that all experiences are unique and a solution for one family is not necessarily the solution for another. Ask yourself what you can contribute to others' journeys. Can you lead a support group? Start one? Consider approaching your church leaders about starting groups in your church. Doing so could be an integral part of your call to care.

If you're going through a journey of your own, participate in a support group not only at the beginning, but throughout.

——— OPENING YOUR HEART ———

- Has reading this chapter changed your thinking about support groups?
- How have you benefited from formal and informal support groups? How did they help?
- What formal or informal support groups do your friends or family access, if any? How have they been helped?
- How might you help fill a need in an existing support group for families and children in your church or community?
- How might you start a support group and for whom specifically? Make a list of steps.

——— PRAYING FOR MY CALL ———

Lord, I'm not sure if a support group is for me to join, participate in, or even lead, if that's your desire. But I'm willing to explore the options and needs in my community and church so you can lead me. Amen.

12

Developing Mentoring Relationships

A good mentor is one of the most valuable assets available to people caring for vulnerable children. The task of caring can be difficult; having a friend along for the journey makes it a bit easier. Early in my career a mentor encouraged me (Bill) to think through the kind of work I wanted to do. This active mentoring helped direct me on the path to my work with Bethany Christian Services.

Over the years I've also had spiritual mentors who helped me through tough spiritual times, mentors who helped my wife and me work through parenting issues, and great friends who have helped us both through the storms of life.

Just as often as I've been mentored, I've mentored others. That's the thing about mentoring—it goes both ways. Each of us has unique knowledge and experience that can help others either in a long-term mentoring relationship or just a talk over coffee.

Mentoring is one of the best ways to help families and children in crisis as well as those who care for vulnerable children and families.

- A mentor is someone who comes alongside to encourage, empathize, and offer understanding. Mentors are companions on the journey.
- The setting can be formal (with a mentor/leader at a church or agency office) or informal (meeting for a meal or snack, sitting at a picnic table in a park).
- The relationship can be formal (hiring a career mentor or as part of adoption or foster care training) or informal (with a friend or acquaintance available to talk).
- The role of a mentor is to be available and listen, listen, listen.

Mentoring Takes Skill

The role of a mentor is to relate to the other person or persons without correcting, to give advice but not jump in to solve everything, and to offer affirmation. Mentoring is about listening and asking questions yet allowing the mentee to come to conclusions and courses of action on their own.

Mentoring isn't directive, but instead it guides through questions and sharing what worked for you or for others you know. It's about asking gentle, open-ended questions and never pushing or shaming.

What differences do you see in how the mentors reacted in these five scenarios?

Scenario 1: Frannie has come to the attention of the state after a complaint was made about possible abuse. Several parents at the children's school reported her screaming at her kids and shoving one of them into a car during after-school pickup. Another parent talked to a teacher after seeing one of Frannie's children with a bruise on her arm.

The school social worker became involved and asked if Frannie might be interested in a mentoring program the school offers to parents. She agreed. They met together for the first time an hour before school released for the day.

"Frannie, how does your day usually go before you pick up the kids?"

"I'm usually coming from caring for my mom, who has cancer. Sometimes the day goes okay; other times it's all about doctors' appointments and I'm running late."

"Do you think sometimes that frustration about running late affects how you are with the kids?"

"I suppose it can. I don't want to be upset with them, but sometimes I'm just so frustrated because I feel like I wasted the day or didn't get anything done."

"I wonder if there are ways you can defuse that frustration before you get to the school."

Scenario 2: The Center family has been going through some rough times financially after losing their catering business. Their three adopted children are in the church youth group, and they've been acting out recently. The older boy got into a fight with another boy, and the daughter was found sobbing in the bathroom during the speaking time at a recent youth gathering. The youngest son refuses to go to church at all; when forced to attend, he sits in the corner, sullen.

The parents are at their wits' end and ask to speak to the youth pastor about what's going on. Here's part of the conversation:

"What's going on at home that might be causing your kids to misbehave?"

"We've lost our catering business, so things have been tight financially as we get back on our feet. We try not to let the kids feel our fears, but maybe they feel like we'll send them back because we can't afford to keep them."

"Obviously. Have you been disciplining them when they act up? Like when your younger son won't go to church?"

"We try, but it seems harsh to spank him when he's so visibly upset. And we were encouraged not to use corporal punishment."

"Children need discipline. I have some rules and disciplines you can set for getting him to come to church."

Scenario 3: A new adoptive mom is concerned that she hasn't bonded with her child, who was eight months old when she and her husband adopted her from China. The child seems content, but the mother fears her own lack of attachment might damage her new daughter. She talks to her adoption specialist at a follow-up visit.

"I feel like I don't love my daughter! I just don't have all those warm, fuzzy feelings other moms talk about after adopting!"

"Why do you think those warm, fuzzy feelings are the only things that indicate love for your child?"

"What should I do to love her more?"

"What do you think are some ways that you already show you love her?"

"But all the other moms . . ."

"I wonder if every mother parents the same way."

Scenario 4: Foster parents are facing some drama at school with their foster children, a sibling group of three elementary and middle school children. The kids seem to be having a tough time with other kids, and they've been caught stealing food. The parents sit down and talk with their foster care specialist.

"We're not sure what to do with the kids. The older one doesn't seem to have any friends, and the little guy was caught stealing food from other kids' lunches and hiding it in his desk."

Over the course of their conversation, the mentor asks the following:

"How do you think the older one might feel about being in a new school? What are some strategies you might share with him about how to be a friend?

"How do you think the younger one's history of trauma and early food insecurity might play into his behavior? How can you reassure him that he'll always have food to eat? It can take a long time for kids to overcome the fear of being hungry; you'll have to be patient."

Scenario 5: An adoptive mom is struggling with unresolved grief regarding her inability to have children. She's thrilled with her new baby yet wonders if they made the right choice to adopt instead of to keep trying to conceive. She talks with her adoption specialist about their plans to adopt again.

"I'm not so sure we should adopt again. What if I get pregnant?"

"Didn't you have all the tests, and you know you can't get pregnant? Don't worry about it."

"But all my friends had their babies the usual way; I'm the only one who didn't."

"So what? You did a wonderful thing, adopting a baby. You're following God's command to care for the least of these. They didn't. Try to get over these feelings before your next placement arrives."

Do you see any difference in how the mentors reacted to the questions? Some were quick to judge, offer solutions, and get on with it. The folks in scenarios 2 and 5 aren't true mentors. The youth pastor in scenario 2 offered only rules and punishment instead of understanding or exploration about how the adopted children might feel as their new family struggles. The adoption specialist in scenario 5 trampled the adoptive mom's grief about not being able to conceive and her questions about next steps.

A true mentor encourages and listens, asks questions and waits to hear the answers, and helps guide the mentee to find answers on his or her own. Adoptive and foster parents, refugees, and care workers—and even adopted children—can benefit from engaging in a mentoring relationship. A mentor can become the safe place to work through struggles and find solutions. Adopted children can especially benefit from interacting with people from their same race and culture.

Both individuals and churches can consider mentoring as one way to care for vulnerable children.

Fahim came to the United States through a refugee program. At eighteen, he couldn't be placed in foster care, but his agency connected him with an older couple, Herb and Kathy, with whom he lived for three years. During that time, he improved his English language skills, began attending church, and enrolled in a community college.

Herb took Fahim under his wing. He helped him practice English as they talked about a possible career path. They explored several options via a career counselor and aptitude tests, and Fahim eventually decided on computer programming.

Herb and Fahim talked about everything, from Fahim's life in a refugee camp to getting a job, from dating to cooking. Herb became the father Fahim had lost years before to war in his homeland.

Fahim moved into an apartment during college, later graduating with a degree in computer programming.

"I wouldn't be where I am today if Herb hadn't helped me figure things out and encouraged me to move ahead in my life," he said.

● ● ●

Jasmine was a single mom with two little girls, and she struggled to find permanent housing. She heard about Safe Families for Children while in a temporary shelter and called to request care for her daughters while she found housing and, hopefully, a job. The girls were placed with Nathan and Breanna.

Breanna and Jasmine bonded over love for the children, and soon they became friends. After Jasmine secured a job and a place to live, she and Breanna had discussions about such things as workplace behavior and school options for the girls.

The informal mentoring Jasmine received from Breanna was vital to her growth as a mom and a person.

OPENING YOUR HEART

- Who has mentored you? What did you gain in that mentoring relationship?
- How have you mentored others over the years? What worked and what didn't?

- How might you mentor newly adoptive parents, foster parents, those struggling with infertility, refugees, or vulnerable children?
- What skills do you need to develop to begin mentoring?
- How do you think you could gain those skills?
- Do you have the time to mentor on a regular basis?

────── Praying for My Call ──────

Lord, is mentoring an answer to the call to care you want me to give? Show me how. Show me whom you would like me to mentor. Give me the courage, wisdom, and confidence I would need for a mentoring relationship with an adult or child who needs one. And if I need to be mentored before I can mentor, show me that too. Amen.

13

Providing Respite Care

The call to care for vulnerable children doesn't necessarily mean a full-time commitment. Your call may be to provide foster parents, adoptive parents, or even birth parents a short-term break when they need it most. You can become part of the team that helps them parent their children.

Parents typically create their own breaks in the form of hiring babysitters for an evening, exchanging childcare with friends, or asking grandparents to care for the grandkids for a day or two at a time. When parenting children who have trauma histories, physical limitations, or special needs, however, finding appropriate care for them can be difficult.

Respite—for Parents

Dr. Karyn Purvis, whom we mentioned earlier, was a strong advocate for finding or offering help to come alongside parents of, as she called them, children from hard places. She suggested respite care so that parents can regroup.[1] Regrouping can mean talking, praying, sleeping, reading, walking, or doing whatever allows them to quiet their hearts and minds.

Rest assured that asking for respite care isn't about disliking the child or children, or about the parent's parenting skills. It's about needing a little space and self-care.

Most important is to make sure children don't feel shame that their parents need a break or feel like they're being punished when their parents leave or allow others to care for them. Appropriate language can alleviate those fears and feelings.

Think about how each of these statements might make a child feel:

"We need a break from you kids. Grandpa and Grandma are going to come over, so we can get away by ourselves."

"We love you so much! Mom and Dad need to spend a little time together, and so Grandma and Grandpa want to spend time with you. You are going to have so much fun!"

One family adopted a child with significant sensory issues. She was often distraught and hysterical. The family, with two other children, sent that one child off for respite care one weekend a month. She knew she was being sent away so the family could rest. Her feelings of inadequacy haunted her, leading to even more difficult behaviors.

Respite—for Children

Respite care can also be about meeting the child's need for space or even individual attention. A foster child may feel overwhelmed by the other children in the home and need alone time or need

---

Respite-In and Respite-Out Care

Respite-in care means the child or children stay in the home with caregivers coming in for short or longer periods of time. Traditional *respite-out* care is when the child or children are cared for outside the home.

---

time and space to grieve not living with her mom any longer. A new parent may need space from responsibilities for their other children to focus on the newest child in the family. Children from hard places sometimes need respite as much as the adults do. The goal is always to build connection.

Whether for a short length of time or for longer periods, respite care is about giving everyone space without interfering with attachment. It's about allowing adults and children space without breaking those growing and often fragile bonds between them.

The Difference between Foster Respite Care and Adoption Respite Care

Foster respite care and adoptive respite care look a little different. Most states are fine with foster parents finding care for a few hours—think date night or grocery shopping—but states may require the care provider be licensed as a foster parent for overnight or longer respite stays. States may also require training along with licensing for foster care respite.

Respite care for adoptive families doesn't require licensing and specific training, but caregivers should be aware of any special physical, behavioral, or emotional needs the child might have. Bethany Christian Services asks foster respite providers to be trained and also recognize that the behavior the family is dealing with may not surface during their time with the child. It's vital that respite providers offer no judgments on the family or their desire for respite care.

Respite-In or Respite-Out?

At Bethany, we almost always recommend respite-in before respite-out. Children usually feel more secure and calm in their own home, surrounded by familiar toys, games, and stuffed animals; they like to sleep in their own beds. Respite-in can be short term, such as an evening or an afternoon of in-home care, or it can be longer term, with caregivers coming to the home for a weekend or longer. Parents can stay in the home—without responsibility for child-care—or leave for the allotted time. The former allows parents to keep the child close, but still offers space for the parents to rest, relax, regroup, and regain perspective.

Respite-in is also preferred from a child development perspective. Respite-in doesn't send the message that the child is being sent away or rejected. It can strengthen attachment by keeping the child close. While there are certainly important reasons for respite-out care, we encourage parents to consider respite-in care as a first step.

How You Can Help

Consider some of the ways you might offer respite-in or respite-out care for families and vulnerable children:

- Take a meal to a foster or adoptive family.
- Offer to pick up children from school and take them to your home for help with homework and dinner once or twice a month.
- Come into the home for an afternoon to allow Mom and/ or Dad to get out for a while or just take a nap.
- Offer to clean the kitchen and bathrooms and do laundry for a busy parent.
- Invite a child or children on an outing to a park, library, museum, or sporting event or to do other fun things, such as sledding, ice skating, seeing a movie, or swimming.
- Offer to drive foster children to visit their parents, go to the doctor, go to the dentist, or get their hair cut.
- Stay at a foster family's home for a weekend (check licensing requirements first) so the parents can take a short vacation.
- Do some shopping for an adoptive or foster family that they don't have time to do.

- Offer to stay with children with special needs during a church service so parents can worship without worry or interruption.
- Stay with younger children while Mom or Dad picks up older children from school.
- Read and play games with children for an hour while Mom or Dad makes dinner.

Churches can also come alongside families caring for vulnerable children to offer respite care (be sure to tap into young people eager to serve).

- Offer free childcare during Bible studies, small group meetings, and other church-related events.
- Connect and partner with a local agency that provides a full continuum of services to children and families.
- Provide one-on-one helpers during youth group, worship services, Sunday school, or summer events to allow parents to leave their children without worry.
- Provide meals for new foster or adoptive parents several nights a week for a month or make and drop off freezer meals to last a month—provided the family has the freezer space.
- Organize weekly babysitting, lawn care, house cleaning, and/or laundry services for families.
- Raise funds for medical care, foster care costs, and adoption costs for those caring for children joining new families.
- Provide free services by trauma-competent counselors through the church.

The lists can go on and on. Individuals and churches can brainstorm many ways to provide children and their families with as much help as they need. Let's look at some other ways respite care can help.

Anthony and Monique adopted a sibling group of three through foster care. They had participated in all the classes and training, so they knew generally what to expect regarding trauma behaviors, sibling rivalry, and common childhood behavior.

But parenting kids all under the age of ten is a lot of work on a good day, not to mention parenting children who have experienced trauma and are in a new place. Their angry outbursts, crying jags, and fighting were making home life difficult. The couple talked to their adoption specialist about their stress level and how best to handle it.

He suggested in-home respite care. Could Anthony's or Monique's parents come over for an evening, so they could go out to dinner? Friends or other relatives? Could they hire a babysitter for a Saturday afternoon, so Anthony could do some needed house repairs and Monique could visit her favorite antique stores?

Anthony's parents started coming over every Tuesday evening, and the couple hired Monique's teenage cousin to come every other Saturday afternoon. These small breaks were just what they needed to restore their souls, regain equilibrium, and better parent the children who needed them at their best.

• • •

Leah adopted two daughters later in life as a single woman with an established career. She'd always wanted to be a mom, but it just didn't work out that way until her girls arrived two years apart via adoption from China.

Her daughters, ages ten and twelve, loved sports and music and playing video games. They were a fun, rambunctious pair, and Leah occasionally yearned for a quiet weekend at home to relax and watch television uninterrupted. She recognized that her years of living alone made the transition to motherhood a little harder than some women might experience.

Another mom suggested Leah see about her girls staying with her sister for a day or two. The girls' aunt was thrilled to have them out to her hobby farm from Saturday morning to Sunday afternoon. Leah got some much-needed solitude and came to get them feeling refreshed. The girls, rather than feeling sent away, had special time with their aunt and bonded to their extended family.

● ● ●

One family began looking for respite care for their foster daughter with challenging medical needs. They loved to hike and camp, but they knew an outdoor setting far from medical care wasn't safe for her. Through agency help they found a local family thrilled to welcome the child into their home while they enjoyed a weekend of outdoor activity.

They showered their foster daughter with love before they left, with the respite family promising to show her the same affection. The family returned from their weekend refreshed. The little girl was delighted to see them as much as they were thrilled to see her.

——— OPENING YOUR HEART ———

- Do you know anyone who has received respite care? How did it help them?
- Have you ever been helped by some form of respite care? How did it make you feel?
- How do you feel about adoptive or foster parents asking for respite care?
- Based on your availability and giftings, what might you do to offer respite to families caring for foster or adopted children? List three things you can do now and three things you might consider doing later.
- How can your church come alongside adoptive and foster families to provide respite care? List at least six ways you think your congregation could help.

—— PRAYING FOR MY CALL ——

Father, we all need rest, and sometimes we need extra rest. Jesus knew that. Show me how I might be able to provide or support respite for those who care for vulnerable children, so they can be renewed as they answer your call. Amen.

14

Covering Financial Needs

People who express interest in caring for vulnerable children almost always ask about the financial cost, especially those looking into foster care and adoption. Potential foster parents want to know how they'll cover expenses for the additional children in the home. Potential adoptive parents want to know how much money they should save to pay for necessary fees and expenses.

No one can tell you foster care won't cost you a dime or hide the fact that adoption costs. Caring for any child isn't free, and children who have had a hard start in life can have additional needs for services or treatments. But the cost of caring doesn't come close to the worth of lives saved and forever changed by your commitment to quality, professional help and your love.

We're not advocating barging ahead with adoption or foster care without a plan in place. We *are* advocating doing due diligence and asking God for provision and help.

This chapter can't cover everything when it comes to the financial costs related to caring for children through foster care or adoption, and this information is in no way meant to be thorough and final. But here are a few important things to know.

Adoption Costs

Adoption is costly because adoption fees reflect the actual cost of agencies providing the service, whether facilitating the home study, training parents, or supporting families during the waiting period. Fees are based on the actual services provided and often don't fully cover the true costs, which include salaries and benefits for licensed professional social workers. Agencies must also be accredited and licensed, and they are audited on service standards, facilities, and their financial operations.

For intercountry adoptions, fees include those paid to the other country. Most countries also require that you or your spouse travels for the adoption, so there will be airline flights, hotels, food, gifts, and other necessities for overseas travel.

When you can add the child to your health insurance is covered by federal law but also by the type of insurance you have and how the law is interpreted. Always check with your insurance provider in advance. Insurance companies can make no distinction between adopted and biological children. The same coverage limits apply to that child as to all children in your home. It's an excellent plan to check on caps and gaps in your insurance coverage as you consider the needs of your newest child.

Check with your agent to learn when you need to add a child. If your child has special placement needs, they may also qualify for certain other programs to help with medical expenses. Part of your service planning before adoption may include exploring these possibilities.

Foster Care Costs

Foster children in your care are covered by Medicaid, a joint federal and state program that provides health insurance coverage. Reimbursements are paid via the state for health care costs related to foster kids, which can include physicals, immunizations, doctor visits for illness, specialist visits, physical and occupational therapies, counseling, and other needs. But the rates of payment and which providers are approved vary. The state also reimburses foster parents via a daily care rate for non–health care costs, such as food and clothing.

Reimbursements may be low, so be aware that foster parents may incur costs that will not be completely covered or reimbursed. Think things such as pay-to-play sports and uniform fees, strollers, school supplies, school field trip fees, and church trip fees.

Other expenses probably not covered but sometimes necessary for helping children with a history of trauma include massage therapy, homeopathic remedies, stress-soothing music, educational games and toys, and aromatherapy.

Foster kids need to feel as loved and cared for as every other child in the family or neighborhood. How might they feel if other children get new backpacks for school and they get ratty, used backpacks? Or must wear ill-fitting, out-of-style clothing? Or don't have gym shoes for gym class? Foster parents need to understand that while funding may not match expenses, it's still important to treat foster kids as they would their own children.

Where to Find Government Help

Many government programs, such as the Special Supplemental Nutrition Program for Women, Infants, and Children, known as WIC; Supplemental Security Income (SSI) for qualified people over age eighteen; and state and local programs, provide assistance. Every state has different rules and requirements for state-funded programs, and government regulations change. Citywide and countywide aid programs may be available. Most, but not all, have an income eligibility test.

Ways to Secure Funding

Don't let talk of financial matters overshadow your call to care. Time and time again God has provided funding for adoption costs, care costs, and all manner of additional expenses. Here are a few ways funding has been provided:

- GoFundMe campaigns
- Fundraising events such as picnics, auctions, and garage sales
- Individual gifts
- Donations from churches
- Donations to agency programs that provide assistance
- Grants from international, national, and private funds focusing on adoption
- Gift cards for gas, clothing, food, and entertainment

Here are five examples of how families were able to secure the finances they needed to care for vulnerable children.

Adam and Jill dreamed of adopting a daughter from Ethiopia, but when fees and costs began to add up, they applied to receive a grant from a fund created to help defray the costs of intercountry adoptions.

They received the grant and soon were matched with a four-year-old girl. They discovered she had a younger sister, and thanks to the financial help they received, they applied to adopt her too. Soon Adam and Jill were on their way to Ethiopia, where they stayed for two weeks to finalize the adoptions. It wasn't long before their daughters were settled in their forever home in the United States.

● ● ●

Brett and Andrea wanted to adopt through the foster care system and began the licensing process. The couple were foster parents for several children and sibling groups before they became foster parents to two little boys who especially touched their hearts.

By now they knew foster care adoption wouldn't be cost-free, but they knew their call to care included these little boys whose birth parents had lost their right to parent. Brett and Andrea's worker applied for funds through Bethany's programs, which helped defray the costs of the adoptions with a financial grant. Within a year, the boys were in their forever home to stay.

● ● ●

Brooke and Seth knew they couldn't have children biologically, and they wanted to begin the adoption process. But fresh from graduate school, they had little left to save after student loan payments and living expenses.

They began a GoFundMe campaign to raise money for the adoption. They blogged about their adoption dreams and used Facebook and other social media to keep family and friends up-to-date on how the process was going.

They moved ahead as funding became available. Three years after starting their fundraising campaign, they welcomed their first child home.

● ● ●

Haley and Gavin became foster parents for a child with special needs who required doctor visits, physical therapy, occupational therapy, and several medications. The child received Medicaid, and the foster parents received subsidies from the state, but the reimbursements weren't high enough to cover all her medications, food for her special diet, and so on.

Haley searched for other funding sources and received some help through grants, and then she approached her church. The church was actively involved in care for at-risk children and was able to fill in the gap between reimbursements and actual costs for the six months the little girl lived with them.

● ● ●

Natalie and Connor adopted two sisters through the foster care system to add to their family, which included three other children. The girls, ages five and eleven, had both experienced trauma before coming into the foster system, and their adoption had come only after protracted attempts at reunification with their birth mother.

Once the girls were officially placed with them, Natalie and Connor added them to their health insurance policy and began taking them to a counselor, a music therapist, and, for the oldest girl, a tutor to catch her up to her peers educationally. The counseling was covered by insurance, but music therapy and tutoring were not. Once school started, the seventh grader received help via the school. Natalie and Connor paid for the extra out of their own pocket.

If You Want to Give Financial Support

In certain situations, donations to accredited charities or non-profits are tax-deductible, though you can't specify a donation going to a specific family. Check on the tax status before making any donation and check with your tax professional to make sure your donation meets the charitable donation definition or requirements of the IRS. Under current regulations, donations through places like GoFundMe are not tax-deductible. Many organizations financially help families.

Meet Georgianne and Don, who found helping financially was their answer to the call to care.

Georgianne and Don felt the call to care for children at risk, but they didn't think adoption or foster care was right for them. With a more-than-adequate income, especially now that their children were married and away from home, the couple used their resources to help families in need.

They began donating to a special adoption agency fund and to their church's fund for needy families, and when they learned of specific needs, they would donate anonymously to help a family.

They were careful to keep track of donations, and they talked to their accountant, so they'd know which donations were tax-deductible. Over fifteen years Georgianne and Don helped close to a hundred families caring for vulnerable children.

───── OPENING YOUR HEART ─────

- Do you think your call to care might be helping to defray the costs of adoption and foster care for others? Why or why not?
- If you're able, how might you specifically help others with those additional costs?
- If you're considering foster care, how do you think your personal finances would come into play?
- If you're considering adoption, how do you think you would fund the adoption?
- Is your church set up to provide funds for families caring for vulnerable children? If not, how might it begin helping in that way?

───── PRAYING FOR MY CALL ─────

God, caring for vulnerable children and families can be costly, but what is the cost if those who can help financially do not? Grant me the means and compassion to give as you wish me to give, in whatever way you want me to give. Amen.

PART FOUR

ENRICHING FAMILY TIES

15

Gaining Support from Others

No matter how a family is created, the world of the child is never just about the nuclear family. Family is about grandparents, aunts, uncles, cousins, and in the case of a child in foster care or who has been adopted, the birth family. And in the best of all worlds, close friends, neighbors, and the people in churches and small groups are "family" too.

Family offers emotional, physical, monetary, and spiritual support to those who answer the call to care. They may not be called to adopt or foster themselves, but they are called to help those in their circle who are.

Acceptance

It is very important that extended family accept and build connection with a child or children who join the family through foster care or adoption. This acceptance provides a sense of belonging to the child and that child's family. How would a family feel if they were excluded from reunions or holiday gatherings because they had adopted a child of another race or country of origin? Or if foster children were excluded from family gatherings or treated differently because they "aren't really part of the family"?

Imagine how a child would feel if she heard this conversation about her:

"Are these your grandchildren?"

"Yes, these are my biological grandchildren, and this is my adopted grandchild."

It may not seem too bad to do so on the surface, but singling out that child as adopted can create feelings of being different, of not being enough, of not being part of the family. Adopted children may struggle with these feelings already; labeling them as different makes it worse. The emphasis should be placed on accepting and integrating children into the family by all members.

Parents—adoptive or foster—need to be alert to subtleties within the extended family and educate the family about the messages they send. Most of the time they don't realize those messages might be divisive or hurtful, but occasionally they do. That's when it's time to have a serious talk or avoid that person altogether if they don't change.

Examples of subtle, perhaps unrealized, behaviors or assumptions abound: a child who was adopted is always last in line for treats; family members assume foster children don't like school or aren't capable of good grades; foster children get secondhand clothing while other children get new clothes; foster or adopted children are left out of conversations or ignored; family members make comments about race or ethnicity.

Reacting to Behavior

Some family or friends may want to make challenging behavior in children be about their adoption or that they are in foster care. But not all behaviors are because of adoption or foster care. It's not family members' jobs to pass judgment on or attempt to determine the reasons for the behavior. They need to love the child and let the parents seek help to figure out behavior if they need to.

Family should be the safest place for vulnerable children who have experienced physical and emotional trauma over which they have no control, and who may act out the traumas to which they have been exposed. As with most of us, behavior can be their clearest voice.

Intrusive Questions

Intrusive questions can come from family members and friends just as much as they can come from strangers. Sometimes you'll need to take the time to answer them seriously if it means protecting your child. But other times the best way to respond is either by not really responding at all or using humor—with a smile, of course. And just because someone asks a question doesn't mean you have to answer it.

"Is that the niece who was adopted?"
"They're all just my nieces and nephews."

"Why are you fostering so many children?"
"How many is too many?"

"Why would you adopt a special-needs child? It's hard enough to care for a child of your own like that, much less someone else's."
"This is my child, and I'm blessed to be her mother."

"Why would you ever adopt a child from overseas?"
"Well, that's where our son was."

"Are all these kids your grandchildren?"
"Yes. Every one of them!"

Each situation where such questions are asked is different, so it's necessary to be aware of the personality of the person asking, your level of relationship, and what is appropriate for them to know. A genuinely curious good friend has different motives than a person known for his or her sharp tongue. A fellow foster parent asking a question is different from a mom who sees her children as a reflection of herself. Answering a question from your caring and generous father-in-law is different from answering one from someone you are barely acquainted with and who is known for being opinionated and gossipy.

Some people need to be educated on adoption and foster care, and this is your opportunity to help them understand. Also, you'll be helping many children who otherwise would be hurt by intrusive comments and questions.

Children especially ask about differences. When a child asks why, for instance, your child is in a wheelchair or has a skin color different from theirs, answer as honestly and positively as possible. Chances are they'll say, "Oh" and then ask your child to play. (As an adult, however, a good rule of thumb is this: If you must ask if a question is appropriate, don't ask the question.)

How Families Can Be Supportive

Here are some ideas for how families can wrap their arms around those who are parenting or otherwise caring for vulnerable children:

- Provide meals, gift cards, and gas cards
- Offer to drop children off at and pick them up from school or school activities
- Provide respite-in or respite-out care
- Offer to babysit so parents can have a night out
- Donate to an adoption fund for a family member
- Take school-age children to purchase school supplies or school clothes
- Take teenagers to sporting events, the movies, or other activities
- Pay for pay-to-play sports fees and/or uniforms
- Attend doctor appointments with a family member to help with a child with medical or emotional needs

Family members play a vital role in caring for vulnerable children. Their call to care through help, prayer, and love is just as important as the call to adopt, foster, or provide other forms of care.

The next two stories are wonderful examples of how special relationships can form between children new to a family and extended family, both for the benefit of the child and parent.

Michael, a child who was biracial, was adopted by a loving family when he was five years old. He was old enough to realize he looked different from his family, who were white, and by the time he was eight years old he was beginning to feel self-conscious about that.

About that time his uncle Trevor came home from military deployment in Afghanistan, where he lost a leg when an IED (improvised explosive device) took out the jeep he was riding in. Michael and Trevor began to form a bond, at first over feeling different and later over a mutual love of video games and of fishing.

The pair became inseparable as Michael grew older, each helping the other understand that they were deeply loved and that their "differences" meant nothing to each other or to the family that loved them. They could also acknowledge to the other that being loved in their family didn't shield them from stares or questions, but it did give them a haven of safety.

● ● ●

Grandpa Stan was a quiet man, but one whose words carried weight with his large family. He and Grandma Emily had passed on their love for caring for others to their six children, with several of them adopting children and several more becoming foster parents.

Family gatherings were loud and fun. Louis became part of the family when he was adopted through foster care by one of Stan's daughters. Louis always stayed back during family gatherings, a peripheral member of the mob of more than twenty-five grandchildren.

During a family picnic, Grandpa Stan saw Louis sitting on the bench during a rousing softball game. He sat down next to the boy and began to tell him about his own childhood. Grandpa Stan's dad left the family during the Depression to find work, and they never saw him again. Stan lived with an aunt and uncle on their farm for a while, and then with an older cousin in the city.

"I know what it's like to lose my family. I know what you're going through," he said.

They sat quietly for a couple of minutes. Then Louis put his hand in his grandpa's hand and held on tight. Grandpa held on tight too.

Soon the softball game was over, and everyone headed to the house for watermelon and lemonade. Before long Louis began to open up to his parents and become part of the cousin uproar when they got together. He and Grandpa Stan had a special bond from that day on.

● ● ●

Rafael had endured severe physical abuse in his birth home. He didn't smile and didn't trust or know how to be comfortable around others, much less accept that he was lovable. Enter Ethan and April, who had been content with just each other in their twenty-year marriage. Then their close friends adopted an older child, and they began to consider it for themselves.

They were prepared as foster parents by their agency, the state issued them a license, and soon eight-year-old Rafael came to visit. Then he stayed for longer periods of time, and permanent placement followed.

Rafael has two sets of grandparents, multiple aunts and uncles, and a host of cousins who all love him and with whom he has formed some special relationships. A boy who once couldn't trust the adults in his life to protect him now has the joy of being part of a loving extended family.

Relatives also have additional insight into their family members' likes, wants, and needs. They can use that insight to bless them as part of their call to care.

Isabelle and Abigail were adopted by Pam, a single mom in her forties. She loved those girls and they loved her, but sometimes she just got tired. Pam's sister Carol had a house full of children and a huge yard with a pool, trampoline, swing set, and garden. There was always something going on, whether board games or hide-and-seek, garden work or races in the pool.

Carol recognized that Pam occasionally needed a break, and for Carol, having two more kids around wasn't a big deal. Chaos is chaos, she liked to say. Every couple of months, Carol invited Isabelle and Abigail to her house for a weekend. The girls loved it, their cousins loved having someone else to play with, Carol loved offering respite to her sister, and Pam relished the time to herself.

Finally, it is good to recognize that family support is important for birth parents as well.

Stephen and Dawn were identified as potential adoptive parents by a young pregnant woman who had decided on an adoption plan. After baby Justin was born, they got the call to come to the hospital. The birth mother's parents and grandparents, both biological and adoptive, were also there. You see, that birth mother had been adopted herself, and she had the support of not only her adoptive mom and dad, but of her birth family as well.

Communicating with children who join new families via foster care or adoption takes time and patience, and no one truly understands what they are feeling, but compassion and caring go a long way toward communicating love. With time, kids can come to understand the love of their new family and love them in return, even as they love their first families.

──────── OPENING YOUR HEART ────────

- Have you ever been hurt by what others have said about you or your family because you were somehow different? How does that memory help inform your compassion for others who are treated the same way?

- How might your own hidden prejudices or preconceived ideas be reflected in your attitude and behavior toward children who are "different" and families that may have been formed differently?
- How might you assist family members or friends caring for children who, because of history, appearance, or behavior, are at risk of exclusion? Look at the list above or make your own list.
- How do you think you might deflect intrusive questions from acquaintances and family members, either on your behalf or that of others?
- How do you think you might best protect any children in your care from uncaring or clueless attitudes from others?

———— PRAYING FOR MY CALL ————

God, thank you for my family and friends and for any help they'll offer me as I explore what your call to care might mean for me, and perhaps for them. Help me, too, be aware of how I can protect others from hurt and to beware of ways I might thoughtlessly hurt children who already feel different. Amen.

16

Developing Provision from the Church

As explained in chapter 1, the Bible is clear that God's people—his church—are called to care for others. And because the church can respond to the call to care in so many ways, it's no wonder this chapter is the longest in this book. Still, although many churches answer this call, some don't.

Our hope is that this chapter can help church members and their leaders see how they can begin to answer God's call to care with the resources they have or can gain.

How Well Do Churches Answer the Call Now?

With the biblical call to churches to look after widows and orphans, it's no surprise that the church at large has spearheaded what has been called the "orphan movement"—the movement to provide orphans around the world with forever homes. That movement has broadened as education on the topic has deepened to include all at-risk children, including those who may still have a living parent or parents unable to care for and protect their children for any number of reasons.

Jedd Medefind is president of the Christian Alliance for Orphans. He is also author of the Barna Group's FRAMES series volume *Becoming Home*, where he provides statistics that indicate Christians are more likely to become foster parents or adopt a child than the general population.

Medefind writes, "Adoption, foster care and other ways of aiding vulnerable children represent vital engagement with a critical social justice need. But they also offer a rich theological expression of our relationship with God. So it only makes sense that Christians would be the first to champion the cause of orphans around the globe."[1] Yet Medefind revealed that survey responses about how well participants thought churches are responding to this call were mixed.

The Local Church

The local church is the perfect place to offer the love and compassion of Jesus Christ to vulnerable children and families nearby as well as around the globe. Every church can understand and work out its calling as well as help believers learn how they can work out their own call to care through the church.

The call to care boils down to what each church and member of that church community can do for each family and each child in need in their sphere of influence. The church becomes a restorative, safe, and welcoming place for families with foster children, children with special needs, new adoptive families, refugee families, families struggling to stay together, and children whose families have dissolved. Every child's life needs to be protected, including the lives of children who aren't yet born; however, being pro-life means protecting children and families at every age. This, too, is the church's responsibility.

When the church accepts that responsibility, church becomes the place to hear "How can we welcome your child?" instead of

"We don't think your child should be in Sunday school," and to hear "How can we help?" instead of "We're sorry, but we have nothing for you here." Church becomes a haven for help without guilt or judgment, without strings or stipulations. The church becomes a home for a family that has fled war, famine, or violence or needs help to overcome poverty or life circumstances keeping them from thriving.

Churches can also contribute to the community at large by spearheading efforts to help those with food and housing insecurity. Helping these folks crosses into helping children, as they are often the most vulnerable in these kinds of situations.

Here are examples of how churches have made a difference.

Rebecca welcomed her first foster care placement soon after she was licensed. Her small group rallied around her, offering help with meals, housecleaning, and prayer support.

Her first experience galvanized Rebecca to encourage her church to become more involved in the care community. She was asked to lead a committee to explore what the church could do. The church began by offering space for support groups and then moved into actively helping foster families in the area with meals, childcare, and transportation. It wasn't long before the community began seeing that church as truly caring for those in need of love and support, who are too often marginalized.

• • •

A large church on the outskirts of the city stood across the road from a high school long known for low test scores and graduation rates. The church's leadership team asked several teachers in the congregation what it could do to help students. They suggested mentoring and after-school programs for homework help.

Soon the church and the school were working together. Sometimes parents expressed appreciation; other times they were out of the picture. The church expanded its outreach by providing food for needy students and their families through its food bank. Several people became involved in foster care as they learned more about the needs in the community.

As one congregant said, "I didn't realize how much we could help by just opening our minds and hearts to the needs out there."

• • •

One church made a commitment to care for foster and adopted children by helping to care for their families in the community. Children often enter foster care with only the clothes on their backs. The church began providing care bags to foster parents when they received a placement. The bags contained age-appropriate clothing, hygiene items, and toys for each foster child. Infant bags included diapers, wipes, and formula. Bags for older children included underwear, socks, and pajamas. Donations were gathered from the congregation.

They also began providing meals to new adoptive families, delivering two meals a week for four weeks. It organized support groups for people interested in adoption, post-adoptive families, foster care families, and those interested in refugee care. Parenting classes were also added to the list of ways the church reached those in need.

The church became a community hub for caring for families formed through foster care or adoption.

• • •

A church was in an urban area hit hard by job loss, rising housing costs, and a lack of grocery stores. Several people in the church who had seen the neighborhood change over the years chose to dig in and help rather than flee to the suburbs.

They started a food pantry that specialized in providing fresh produce along with fresh dairy items and nonperishable foods. With donations and grants, they installed several refrigerators and a freezer to accommodate the fresh goods. The couples researched programs such as Feeding America to buy fresh and nonperishable food at very low cost. They contacted several local farmers about donating their excess produce.

Among the first to take advantage of the food pantry was a foster family from the church who was caring for three young teenagers but whose food allowance wasn't enough to keep those adolescent stomachs full. They were all grateful for the extra food.

• • •

Austen and Destiny became foster parents to siblings ages seven and four. This was their first placement, and they were a little overwhelmed. They expressed their fears and feelings to their small group from church, which immediately began looking for ways to help. Four couples started by visiting the family on a Saturday afternoon.

The men mowed, weeded, cleaned gutters, and washed both cars. The women cleaned the house and washed, folded, and put away laundry. Austen and Destiny watched in amazement as the couples swooped in, did their work, and drove away waving. Pizza was delivered for the family twenty minutes later.

A Checklist for Churches

Like the checklists in chapter 4, here's a checklist that can help churches assess their capabilities and resources and prepare when

Accepting Help as a Caregiver

Much help is available for you as a caregiver, but you must accept that help.

Some families feel like they should do this on their own, that answering the call to care the way they have was their decision and therefore solely their responsibility. This couldn't be further from the truth. Caring for vulnerable children and families is a job for all of us. Accepting help is just as important as offering it. Care for yourselves as well as you care for others in your home or wherever you serve.

they're called to care for vulnerable children, especially within their own walls.

Caring by the Church

- Determine steps to educate and inform the congregation about the families and children to be supported in a compassionate and caring manner.
- Determine who will lead. A church can have a staff member dedicated to coordinating efforts in this area, one person who makes decision-making more effective and signals to the congregation and community that this is a church that cares.
- Train volunteers and staff dedicated to welcoming families with children who have special needs, qualified caregivers for children with special needs, and adults to deal with issues unique to traumatized teens and young adults.
- Renovate classrooms, bathrooms, hallways, and so on to accommodate wheelchairs and other equipment. Nothing signals "stay away" more than facilities that don't accommodate wheelchairs, walkers, canes, and so on. A church staff point person can advocate for renovation funding to meet these needs. When building or renovating, think carefully about what people with special needs might need.
- Equip classrooms for kids with special needs, including those with physical disabilities and emotional and developmental delays. Sensory rooms are safe places for children with sensory processing challenges and other special needs to go to regulate their emotions or take a break from noise, activity, and other stimuli. Sensory rooms need appropriate lighting, toys, play equipment, and supervision.
- Stock appropriate toys and play equipment. Welcoming all children means having toys that reflect their needs. Dolls of all colors, books with children of all colors and races,

crayons representing all skin colors, and teaching materials that show kids of all colors are all necessary. Churches should have toys appropriate for children with physical disabilities, sensory processing challenges, and other needs.

- Obtain curricula and other materials appropriate for families who don't speak English as a first language and for children with special needs.

What Else the Church Can Offer

Here are some of the other ways churches can make a difference.

Support Groups

Churches can offer space for a variety of groups to meet to discuss needs and care-related issues and to share information. Support groups can cater, for instance, to domestic or intercountry adoption, foster care or foster care adoption, care for and adoption of children with special placement needs, infertility support, unplanned pregnancy support, or refugee support.

Mentorship Programs

Churches can connect people who can mentor and who need mentoring, including adults who can give teenagers in foster care educational or life skills support, parents who can be mentored by other parents, experienced adoptive families who can mentor new adoptive families, and those who need financial mentoring or cultural mentoring who can be mentored by others in the church. The opportunities for mentoring children and families facing challenges are many.

Practical Support

Churches can be the hub for a network that provides practical support for vulnerable children and families. These families can include foster parents, adoptive parents, refugee families, respite-care volunteers, women with unplanned pregnancies, or foster and adoptive families of children with special needs.

Here are some ideas to get you started on your own creative list:

- Take meals or supply groceries to new adoptive families or foster parents with a new placement.
- Clean the house or do laundry for a busy parent.
- Stay with the children while their parents go out for an evening of much-needed time alone.
- Offer to pick children up from or drop them off at school.
- Provide respite-in or respite-out care.
- Provide gift cards to area stores, restaurants, or gas stations.
- Do lawn care, such as mowing, raking leaves, or weeding.

Helping Has Some Caveats

Do you know what Jesus said in Matthew 6:2–3 about giving to the needy? He said, "Do not announce it with trumpets, as the hypocrites do in the synagogues and on the streets, to be honored by others. . . . But when you give to the needy, do not let your left hand know what your right hand is doing."

The kernel of this teaching applies to *how* you help those in need. Providing help requires a certain etiquette. If you go to a home, don't linger without being asked and be sensitive to the cues the family is giving. Leave when it's time to leave, and even before it's obviously time to leave.

For example, dropping off a meal with a family who just received a foster care placement is not the time for a social call. Don't expect to be asked in, and don't expect to be honored and lauded for your meal. Keep to yourself how long it took you to make it or how much the ingredients cost. Simply say hello, leave the meal, and go. We need to show up, not show off.

Some people leave the meal in a cooler outside the back door or provide a gift card to a takeout place or restaurant with delivery service with the menu attached.

Consider, too, the kinds of food children generally like. Highly spicy food probably isn't going to be appreciated, and maybe that fancy artichoke heart casserole with Gouda cheese won't be a hit with the younger crowd. Among favorites are pizza and bread sticks, spaghetti, the makings of a taco bar, a bucket of chicken and fixings, and a gallon of ice cream and some brownies for dessert.

Be sensitive to any dietary restrictions you know about and to cultural taboos if you're providing food to refugees or newly adopted children from another culture. Many refugees aren't used to eating certain meats or any meats. If in doubt, ask.

Another caution concerns martyrdom. Don't moan and groan about how much work it is to provide help to the refugee family your church is sponsoring. If you feel you must tell your friends how much time and money you spent on the foster family, rethink doing it in the first place. Offering help is deeply important; doing so with a boastful or martyred heart still gets food to the needy but may harm them and you in the process. Our role is to walk alongside.

Ask Families How the Church Can Help

A best practice for churches is to sit down with families and ask how the church can help them. Those families may have never been asked and can offer unique insights into not only physical needs but also how they perceive the church feels about them. They could be families in your community who had children with special needs born to them or who fostered or adopted them. Do people greet them as they walk in with their child in a wheelchair? Are they constantly called out of the worship service when their child or foster child exhibits dysregulated behavior such as meltdowns or aggression? Are they invited to church or small group events? Do they feel like their child is adequately cared for in the nursery or classes?

Here's how some churches stepped up to the plate, but they had to open their ears and eyes to know the needs before they could meet them.

Nabil and Rima brought their family to the United States from a war-torn country through a Christian agency's refugee program. The church sponsoring them, with one of its small groups on point, had done their homework so they'd know what the family's needs were likely to be.

One small-group member, a real estate expert, found them an affordable apartment. Donations of household goods, beds and bedding, and cleaning and hygiene supplies rounded out the pre-arrival preparations. Once the parents and three children arrived in the United States, however, the church asked them about their needs, and others stepped up to help them apply for the services they both needed and wanted, such as food assistance, translation services, health care, English tutoring, and government-issued IDs. They also learned more about the food the family would like to eat and tried to provide meals catering to those preferences.

● ● ●

Kent and Julie adopted a child with special needs through domestic adoption. They loved their son, but they struggled with keeping up with him and their other obligations. Finally, they mentioned their struggles to their Sunday school class at church.

The group went into action. First, they prayed for Kent and Julie and committed to continue praying for them every day. Second, they asked what they needed specifically. The pair said they could use a little time away to refresh and relax. Several couples in the group committed to coming over one night a week for several hours so the new parents could have a dinner out. Others offered once-a-month care on a Saturday to give them respite.

Julie and Kent were so grateful they cried. These small services helped them get through a difficult adjustment time.

Help People Discover How They Can Help through the Church

Caring in a church isn't simply filling an empty spot with a body to get a job done. When churches allow people to try different areas of service without judgment, individuals can determine the best fit where they can help. For instance, with guidance from experts, churches can offer classes on how to care for children with sensory processing challenges or how to understand and deal with behaviors in foster children that resulted from trauma.

A friend of mine (Bill's) knew God was calling him to care for vulnerable children, but he didn't know how that would look for him. He tried working with children with physical disabilities but didn't feel comfortable. He tried delivering meals to families with new foster children, but his work schedule was too unpredictable. What he found he was best at and enjoyed most was one-on-one interaction during the church service with a child who had a trauma background or who had challenges processing stimuli such as noise, touch, or movement.

Every other week for a year he played with, read to, or rocked a four-year-old boy so his foster parents could attend the worship service. They became great friends, that traumatized little boy beginning to heal thanks in part to the attention and love from his gentle friend. Later he sat in the sensory room with a three-year-old girl and read to or played with her. He watched her make progress over time.

His church had formed a mission and vision for caring for vulnerable children and put appropriate safeguards and protocols in place to protect them and all children. This allowed him to find the best outlet for his call to care. He continues that call to this day, now having helped care for nearly a dozen children. He's quick to say that they helped him more than he ever helped them. He still counts those children and their parents as friends.

Encourage your church to investigate how members can serve in the Safe Families for Children program, which you've seen featured several times in this book, or something like it. An agency such as

Bethany oversees the program locally, recruiting churches that then recruit families and host training. This isn't a foster care situation requiring licensing and state oversight to care for those in danger of abuse or neglect, but a place for families that need temporary care for their children and compassion.

The church has a wide-open door to become a vital hub of care for vulnerable children, with opportunities to encourage, train, and facilitate volunteers to work out their individual calls to care. And through offering options such as support groups and care during services, the church can also encourage families who care for children who have more challenges than others to be part of the body of Christ.

Not all opportunities to serve involve families who share or even know about Christian beliefs, however. Many have no religious background or leanings at all. Some are of other faiths.

One church sponsored a refugee family from Syria, who were Muslim. A small group took the lead, searching out housing, taking care of meals, and finding furniture and household goods for them. Three of the small-group women organized meals, while others guided the family to connect with social services and non-profit groups to help them navigate the health care, educational, and social service arenas, as well as employment opportunities. Many Muslim families have shared how Christian families have loved them, cared for them, and invited them to church.

God expects no less than our reaching out to others who need our help, no matter their country of origin or religious beliefs.

OPENING YOUR HEART

- How has your thinking about caring for vulnerable children through your church changed as you've read this book and this chapter?

- Does your church effectively welcome children with special needs and their families? If so, how?
- How is your church doing with the call to care overall? How can you help your church answer or expand its call?
- How do you think your church can help you and others find the best fit serving in the church's call to care?
- Look over your church's teaching materials, toys, books, and games. Do they serve children of different abilities, races, cultures, and skill levels? How can they be adjusted to serve all children?

———— PRAYING FOR MY CALL ————

Lord, your church—your people—are called to help the vulnerable around us. Help me be more aware and open to how my church can be challenged to answer the call to care for vulnerable children and families, and how I in turn can serve them. Amen.

17

Accessing Assistance from the Community

Professional community resources—in communities both large and small—are a vital part of the care for children who have experienced trauma or have physical, developmental, or emotional challenges. Without the professional community, many parents and caregivers would be without an important safety net and crucial services that help vulnerable children become as emotionally, physically, and mentally healthy as they can be.

For those who follow Christ, there is no shame in or rule against using the community services that recognize the need to care for children.

Exploring What's Available

Here are some ways anyone who is considering caring for a vulnerable child can search out helpful resources:

- Identify physicians and pediatricians who have experience with children who are living in foster care, have been adopted domestically or internationally, and have experienced numerous harmful situations such as malnutrition, disease, or trauma.

- Research educational resources such as Montessori, charter, public, and private schools and early childhood programs that will meet a child's needs, as well as outside educational resources such as private tutors or tutoring programs.

- Find language services for refugee families or adoptive children who come to the United States without English language skills.

- Pinpoint where best to find mental health resources specific to a parent's or child's needs.

- Discover the resources a school district provides pertinent to speech and language, reading, and disability needs.

- Investigate what support subsidies are available for foster children who are wards of the state and in care.

Caregivers Don't Have to Do It All

Caregivers don't have to find a way to meet every need themselves. For instance, they don't have to do everything to help refugees under their care or guidance. They can partner with the community to provide well-rounded care and help through services that already exist. Some churches take advantage of several nonprofit organizations dedicated to helping refugee children with language services, after-school tutoring and homework help, summer day camp programs, or transportation services. Parents are aided by language help, job search help, and job skills training.

One child came into his foster home behind in speech and language skills. The foster parents explored what their neighborhood elementary school could provide and discovered they could take the three-year-old to the school for a half hour of speech therapy twice a week with a certified speech pathologist, at no cost. The child, with a little help, was soon developing language skills at his age level.

The resources available are numerous, depending on where you live, but if services like the ones below aren't available, you can begin advocating for them in your schools and community.

- Language interpreters for education and health care
- Specialty medical clinics for wound care, asthma care, pain care, the feeding of infants with cleft lip and palate, diabetic care, and other specific health issues
- Speech and language development help
- ESL (English as a second language) classes
- Autism spectrum education services
- Early childhood education and intervention services
- Services for the deaf and hearing impaired
- Occupational therapy
- Mental health services, including in-patient and out-patient care and counseling
- Pregnancy care resources
- Parenting classes
- Social service programs with food support, such as WIC (the Special Supplemental Nutrition Program for Women, Infants, and Children) or food stamps
- Food pantries and clothing closets
- Mentoring and tutoring services

If you seek counseling help for your foster child and for you, because counseling works through the family relationship, make sure the counselor is adoption competent. This means that they understand the losses inherent in adoption and the grief that comes with those losses. Clinicians also need to be knowledgeable about trauma and the various kinds that children may have experienced as well as competent in trauma treatment. We are continually learning more about trauma, almost every day, and its impact on the brain.

Consider these searches for professional services:

Shelley and Chip adopted Jesse, who was diagnosed with a sensory processing disorder that caused him to react intensely and melt down when exposed to fluorescent lighting that produced a hum, as well as to other noises such as vacuums and low-flying airplanes. Because many schools have fluorescent lighting, they had trouble finding the right environment for their son.

They connected with a support group for parents of other children with sensory integration problems and soon learned about a school with programs focused on children with sensory processing issues. It was part of their local school district and served kids from the region.

Jesse was soon enrolled. He thrived there, his natural talent for writing and storytelling soon coming out, thanks to a calming environment and teachers who understood his challenges and made modifications to prevent him from being overwhelmed.

• • •

Charlotte and Trey began fostering with a plan to adopt, and soon three siblings were placed in their home. Because the children had a known history of trauma, Charlotte and Trey searched for a pediatrician within the Medicaid insurance plan who had experience dealing with childhood trauma.

A list of pediatricians was given to them by the Medicaid provider, and they did their due diligence by researching each one and asking their adoption agency and other foster parents who they recommended. They found the perfect match: a doctor who loved their kids, whose office was located near them, and who understood how trauma can affect children and how they face medical care.

• • •

Brendon and Cybil adopted their daughter from China. They knew her cleft lip and palate would require several surgeries and that they would face feeding issues when she arrived.

They talked to their family doctor and researched the services offered by a children's hospital in their town. Brendon and Cybil met with
an expert in cleft lip and palate care, who talked to them about what
to expect and showed them around the feeding clinic at the hospital.
They learned how to feed their daughter and what care she would need.

These parents were prepared when their daughter arrived, making
all their transitions smoother.

Paying for Services

One question people often ask is how these services can be paid
for. Sometimes services are free through nonprofits, funded by
the generous donors to those organizations, and school districts
also provide many free services for children in the district. Family
medical insurance has provisions for health and mental health care,
and Medicaid will cover many costs for children in foster care.

Advocates within these fields—often social workers in various
settings—can help you find the resources available to you. For instance, Bethany Christian Services includes community resources
as part of the care plan each family develops preceding adoption
(see more about the care plan in the appendices). One component
of the plan encourages families to learn what services are available
to them in the community. Every parent—adoptive and foster—
assumes responsibility for the child or children, and part of that
is knowing what the needs are and knowing what's available in
the community.

How Communities Can Improve Their Services

Every community can work to improve how families find services
throughout the area and how they can best take advantage of
those services. Some offer online directories and services such as
2-1-1, a hotline staffed by people who can direct callers to the
social services they need.

You may even become part of enhancing your community's care network through your own activities, your church's work, or your work at local government levels to advocate for programs that help vulnerable children.

Here are two stories that illustrate how that can happen:

Jayne had been a licensed foster care provider for several years before starting her own nonprofit to provide care packages to children removed from their homes and newly placed with foster families.

She was contacted by the state agency that placed children in care to let her know the ages and number of children recently placed. Later that day or early the next day (for late-night placements), she would provide a bag to the social worker who dropped it off at the home.

The families of babies and younger children received a homemade blanket, pajamas, diapers, wipes, formula, socks, and perhaps an outfit or small toy—whatever was appropriate for the child's age. Families of older children received hygiene items, pajamas, underwear, socks, a small toy, and other appropriate items.

Jayne gathered the items for her care packages through donations from area churches, schools, businesses, and individuals. One child of a friend of hers asked those coming to her birthday party to bring donations for the packages instead of birthday presents.

Jayne saw a need in the community through her own work, and she created a solution to meet that need.

• • •

Elisa and Jack's daughter Krista and her husband, Matt, were involved in the foster care system as foster parents and mentors for new foster parents. While the older couple didn't feel their call to care involved foster care, they were happy to care for their daughter's charges for short times and were committed to pray for them and other foster families and children.

When their church decided to participate in Safe Families for Children, they were the first to begin praying and helping participating families with meals and gift and gas cards. Their interaction with SFFC led to interactions with nonprofits in the community, such as tutoring and mentoring groups, to which they donated as they could.

Their gifts were returned a hundredfold as lives were changed throughout their city.

————— OPENING YOUR HEART —————

- Do you ever have trouble asking for help when you need it? Why or why not?
- Why do you think it's hard for some caregivers to ask for help?
- Do you know what services are available in your community to assist vulnerable families and children?
- Can you identify a service you feel especially called to support in some way?
- What gaps in community services might your church help fill?

————— PRAYING FOR MY CALL —————

Lord, thank you for the services my community provides and for the partnerships those services, churches, and individuals can form to provide care. Help me find my place in the community to care for vulnerable children and their families. Amen.

Afterword

We hope this book makes it clear that caring for vulnerable children is a job for individuals, families, churches, and whole communities. That care is a love story for people whose lives have taken a turn—perhaps through entering the foster system; having an unintended pregnancy and adoption; dealing with physical, emotional, or mental health needs; or experiencing poverty, war, or famine and relocation to a new country.

We're all called to show Jesus' love to the children and families who need it most. We're all called to care for vulnerable children. That care can be messy and challenging, yet delightful and rewarding. No matter how it looks, that care is a beautiful picture of Christ's love and care for us despite the mess.

We also hope this book has encouraged you to discover what your call to care looks like and how that call can make an impact on the lives of vulnerable children.

May God's love fill both your heart and the hearts of the children you help.

What Is the Bethany Christian Services Continuum of Care?

We live in a broken world, and Bethany has found that the need for family support crosses the economic, social, and racial spectrums. No one should assume that adults—no matter where they live, how much they earn, or the color of their skin—have solid parenting skills. The lack may look different in different places, but the results can be the same: Children experience things in their young lives that teach them they have to protect themselves. Behavior is how children express their needs, no matter how it comes across to the adults around them.

To do the work that we do, Bethany provides services along a continuum of care.

Within Our Borders

On the one end of the continuum are low- to medium-risk families who access preventative care through options such as SFFC (Safe Families for Children), parent coaching, and community services. Higher-risk families may be able to access programs such as HOMEBUILDERS and Intact Family Services. If a child is removed from the home, he or she moves into relative care, foster care, or therapeutic foster care (also called treatment foster care).[1] For children with severe behavioral health conditions, foster parents can be trained to be part of the therapeutic service team for the child. Children with more intense needs may require care outside of a family setting via group homes or residential treatment.

The goal is always to move toward permanence, whether that is through family preservation, reunification, or adoption, and to provide support for the family through post-placement or post-adoption services—whenever the family needs that support.

Our goal is to protect and help families and children who fall anywhere on that continuum, as well as encourage churches and communities to do the same.

Is a family considering adding to their number through adoption? We offer adoption services to help them achieve that goal, including counseling and financial help. Churches can offer adoption support groups, meals, childcare, financial help, and counseling.

Is foster parenting a consideration? Bethany provides training and licensing, and we connect foster parents with children in need. Churches might offer support groups, childcare, meals, supplies, and qualified workers during church services.

Is someone eager to help families avoid their children going into care? They can participate in Safe Families for Children, and

---

1. According to the Family Focused Treatment Association, "Treatment Foster Care is a distinct, powerful, and unique model of care that provides children with a combination of the best elements of traditional foster care and residential treatment centers. In Treatment Foster Care, the positive aspects of the nurturing and therapeutic family environment are combined with active and structured treatment. Treatment Foster Programs provide, in a clinically effective and cost-effective way, individualized and intensive treatment for children and adolescents who would otherwise be placed in institutional settings." This information is quoted from "What is Treatment Foster Care," Family Focus Treatment Association, accessed March 25, 2019, https://www.fta.org/page/DefiningTFC.

their church can offer mentoring services, counseling, and tutoring for children.

God put families in the center of his plan for the world. Our call is to do everything in our power—and we encourage you to do the same—to preserve those families.

Beyond Our Borders

Family preservation takes place far beyond the borders of the United States. Bethany Christian Services, via Bethany Global, is involved in programs around the world that help stabilize families.

We work to preserve families with programs that target the underlying causes of disintegration, including lack of job skills/training, inadequate housing, food insecurity, and lack of clean water. Bethany's Family Preservation and Empowerment program helps thousands of children stay in their families. This program is funded through One Family Sponsorship, which allows families from around the US to support the family-strengthening work Bethany Global does in countries around the world. When parents can no longer afford to care for their children, they often face terrible choices, such as placing children in an orphanage, sending them to the streets to beg instead of to school, dealing with human traffickers, or giving away young daughters in marriage. The reality of their poverty is unbearable for both parent and child. Strengthening families for the well-being of children is our top priority.

My (Bill's) wife, Mary, and I did not adopt or foster. With four biological children, a capacity—emotionally, physically, and financially—was not there to be foster or adoptive parents. However, we were able to sponsor children through Bethany's One Family Sponsorship. We have sponsored more than ten children and experienced each child's life change through the program. Children graduated from high school and families became financially independent. Best of all, these children were able to remain with their parents and siblings.

Along with my husband, I (Kris) also have sponsored families through this program and have watched families "graduate" to self-sufficiency. What I love most about this program is the focus both on keeping families together and empowerment. The goal is to partner with them in accessing the resources they need, building on their existing strengths.

Bethany Global works with indigenous agencies or creates agencies to offer in-home family services and foster care services. The staff are educated with the appropriate degrees and training to perform these services.

Visit www.bethany.org/global/our-work to learn more.

What Is the Bethany Christian Services Family Care Plan for Adoptive Parents?

Bethany Christian Services develops a care plan with families seeking to adopt domestically or internationally, helping them think through resources they may need and locate those resources before they need them. Identifying potential resources not only helps the family think creatively about what support might be available to them, but it makes accessing that support easier and doable *before* the family feels they are in crisis.

Included in the care plan are childcare arrangements, whether for family crises, work, or short times away; support systems, including friends, family, and church community; health care, including medical specialties they may need; interpreters; adoption-competent counselors; and more.

We want to make sure the family has adequate and appropriate supports in place to meet the needs of the child or children and to keep the family strong in times of challenge or stress. The practical side of the call to care is just as important as recognizing the call and appropriately examining motives and expectations.

Recommended Books for Adoptive and Foster Care Parents

Gray, Deborah D. *Nurturing Adoptions: Creating Resilience after Neglect and Trauma*. London: Jessica Kingsley Publishers, 2012.

Gritter, James L. *Hospitious Adoption*. Arlington, Virgina: CWLA Press, 2009.

Keck, Gregory C., PhD, and Regina M. Kupecky, LSW. *Adopting the Hurt Child: Hope for Families with Special-Needs Kids*. Rev. and updated ed. Colorado Springs: NavPress, 2009.

Keck, Gregory C., PhD, and Regina M. Kupecky, LSW. *Parenting the Hurt Child: Helping Adoptive Families Heal and Grow*. Rev. and updated ed. Colorado Springs: NavPress, 2009.

Nydam, Ronald J. *Adoptees Come of Age: Living within Two Families*. Louisville, Kentucky: Westminster John Knox Press, 1999.

Purvis, Karyn B., PhD, David R. Cross, PhD, and Wendy Lyons Sunshine. *The Connected Child: Bring Hope and Healing to Your Adoptive Family*. Columbus, Ohio: McGraw-Hill Professional, 2007.

Roorda, Rhonda M. *In Their Voices: Black Americans on Transracial Adoption*. New York: Columbia University Press, 2015.

Schooler, Jayne E., Betsy Keefer Smalley, LSW, and Timothy J. Callahan, PsyD. *Wounded Children, Healing Homes: How Traumatized*

Children Impact Adoptive and Foster Families. Colorado Springs: NavPress, 2010.

Schooler, Jayne E., and Thomas C. Atwood. *The Whole Life Adoption Book: Realistic Advice for Building a Healthy Adoptive Family.* Rev. and updated ed. Colorado Springs: NavPress, 2008.

Siegel, Daniel J., MD, and Tina Payne Bryson, PhD. *The Whole-Brain Child: 12 Revolutionary Strategies to Nurture Your Child's Developing Mind.* New York: Bantam, 2012.

Acknowledgments

Bill:

I would like to acknowledge all Bethany Christian Services staff, both those currently working and past staff. Bethany staff are compassionate and caring and focus on the protection and well-being of children.

In addition, Bethany staff are committed to providing the best clinical-based service and practices. Bethany has been on the cutting edge of family-based care, foster care, residential care, and adoption. Bethany staff believe in innovation, change, and correcting practices to benefit families and children. Another value expressed by Bethany staff is transparency. This allows Bethany to expose its services and practices to clients, recipients, and other professionals, which helps us continually improve.

To name some Bethany staff but not others would be an injustice. Yet I would like to thank Kris Faasse and Dawn Thompson for their work on this book. Without them this book would not have been possible.

Kris:

This book would never have been were it not for the dedication to Bethany Christian Service's mission and the foresight of Pete

Knibbe, both a friend and long-term colleague at Bethany. He connected us to Verne Kenney, who also had the vision for this book. Once started, I couldn't have done any of it without the support and input of my closest working team: Sarah Horton Bobo, Kristen Meyer, Gregory Kurth, Kristi Gleason, Rebecca Rozema, Kimberly Offutt, Julie Paine, Angela Welch, Carol Lee, Janelle Biemers, and Donna Nicholson, along with George Tyndall and Dona Abbott. Listing colleagues always risks leaving others out, especially since so many of my colleagues over the years have developed programs at Bethany as well as challenged established ways of thinking and the delivery of services. None of us do this work alone, and even if you aren't listed by name, know that you've influenced either my thinking or the thinking of others here. If I could list all of Bethany's team, past and present, I would, because all have had a hand in some way.

The dedication to the work of Bethany was inspired and reinforced by the many families who have allowed us to come alongside them in times of challenge, crisis, and joy. We have learned so very much from you, not only from your experiences but from the candor with which you have shared them with us. You have continually challenged us to see children and families as the beautiful and unique individuals that God created each of us to be. Thank you for your trust in us.

Thank you to Ann Byle for her invaluable assistance in getting this off the ground. And, once the idea was launched, it would not have happened without the constant shepherding and research of Dawn Thompson. Project manager just doesn't cover it all.

To my family, Tom, Todd, Danielle, Sarah, Kate, my kids' spouses who have become our other kids, and my precious four grandsons—without your love and support, I couldn't do the work that I do or give as much time to the work of Bethany as I do. You inspire me and, just by your presence, give me immeasurable joy. Time with you is my place of refuge.

And, finally, because he is the reason for all of this, my thanks to God for allowing me to serve him in this way, to be a little part of his work in so many lives. I am both grateful and humbled.

Notes

Introduction

1. Karyn Purvis, "Children from Hard Places," published by Empowered to Connect, August 17, 2013, video, https://www.youtube.com/watch?v=Qe-BkH UVGQ4.

Chapter 1: What God's Word Says

1. Julie Zauzmer, "Christians Are More than Twice as Likely to Blame a Person's Poverty on Lack of Effort," *Washington Post*, August 3, 2017, https://www .washingtonpost.com/news/acts-of-faith/wp/2017/08/03/christians-are-more-than -twice-as-likely-to-blame-a-persons-poverty-on-lack-of-effort/.

Chapter 3: Determining Expectations

1. The phrase "dance of attachment" is taken from the book *Learning the Dance of Attachment: An Adoptive Foster Parent's Guide to Nurturing Healthy Development* by Holly van Gulden and Charlotte Vick (lulu.com, second ed., 2010).

Chapter 5: A Close Look at Foster Care

1. "Aging Out Initiative," Christian Alliance for Orphans, accessed February 4, 2019, https://cafo.org/aging-out/.

2. Quoted from Sebilu Bodja, "Every Child, Everywhere," *LifeLines*, Summer 2017, 14–15, http://bethany-christian-services.dcatalog.com/v/2017-Summer-Life Lines/?page=14.

Chapter 6: A Close Look at Adoption

1. Chuck Johnson, introduction to *Adoption by the Numbers*, by Jo Jones and Paul Placek, ed. Chuck Johnson and Megan Lestino (Alexandria, VA: National Council for Adoption, 2017), ii.

2. US Department of State—Bureau of Consular Affairs, *Fiscal Year 2017 Annual Report on Intercountry Adoption*, https://travel.state.gov/content/travel /en/Intercountry-Adoption/adopt_ref/adoption-publications.html.

3. Children's Bureau, *The AFCARS Report*, August 2018, https://www.acf.hhs .gov/sites/default/files/cb/afcarsreport25.pdf.

4. *Safeguarding the Rights and Well-Being of Birthparents in the Adoption Process* (New York: Evan B. Donaldson Adoption Institute, November 2006, revised January 2007), 11 and 52, https://www.adoptioninstitute.org/old/publica tions/2006_11_Birthparent_Study_All.pdf.

5. "NBC Announcer Says He Regrets Tweet about Simone Biles' Parents," *Chicago Tribune*, August 8, 2016, https://www.chicagotribune.com/sports/inter national/ct-al-trautwig-simeone-biles-twitter-20160808-story.html.

Chapter 7: A Closer Look at Domestic Adoption

1. Children's Bureau, *The AFCARS Report*, August 2018, https://www.acf.hhs .gov/sites/default/files/cb/afcarsreport25.pdf.

Chapter 8: A Closer Look at Intercountry Adoption

1. US Department of State—Bureau of Consular Affairs, *Fiscal Year 2016 Annual Report on Intercountry Adoption*, https://travel.state.gov/content/travel/ en/Intercountry-Adoption/adopt_ref/adoption-publications.html.

2. Karyn B. Purvis, David R. Cross, and Wendy Lyons Sunshine, *The Connected Child: Bring Hope and Healing to Your Adoptive Family* (New York: McGraw-Hill, 2007), 1–2.

Chapter 9: Acknowledging Loss and Grief

1. Kenneth J. Doka, PhD, "Is There a Right to Grieve?" *Psychology Today*, November 30, 2018, https://www.psychologytoday.com/us/blog/good-mourning /201811/is-there-right-grieve.

2. Pauline Boss, "Ambiguous Loss Theory: Challenges for Scholars and Practitioners," *Family Relations* 56, no. 2, (April 2007): 105–110.

Chapter 13: Providing Respite Care

1. Lisa Qualls, "How We Found Help in the Midst of Crisis," *Empowered to Connect*, accessed March 25, 2019, empoweredtoconnect.org/how-we-found-help -in-the-midst-of-crisis/.

Chapter 16: Developing Provision from the Church

1. Jedd Medefind, *Becoming Home* (Grand Rapids, MI: Zondervan, 2014), 20.

Bill Blacquiere served Bethany Christian Services for thirty-two years as chief operating officer, director of operations for Michigan, and most recently CEO, retiring at the end of 2017. He also served on the boards of the National Council for Adoption and the Christian Alliance for Orphans. He and his family live in Grand Rapids, Michigan.

Kris Faasse, LMSW, ACSW, is senior vice president of clinical operations for Bethany Christian Services. A recognized adoption expert, Kris has provided training in national and international settings and authored numerous articles. She also has served on various boards, including Justice for Our Neighbors–Michigan, which serves refugees and immigrants with low-cost or free legal services. She lives with her family in Grand Rapids, Michigan.